CLAUDIAN'S PANEGYRIC ON THE FOURTH CONSULATE OF HONORIUS

LIVERPOOL LATIN TEXTS
(CLASSICAL AND MEDIEVAL)
2

CLAUDIAN'S PANEGYRIC ON THE FOURTH CONSULATE OF HONORIUS

Introduction, Text, Translation
and Commentary

by

WILLIAM BARR

FRANCIS CAIRNS

Published by Francis Cairns
The University, P.O. Box 147, Liverpool L69 3BX,
Great Britain.

FIRST PUBLISHED 1981

ISBN 0 905205 11 1

Printed in Great Britain by
Redwood Burn Limited, Trowbridge, Wiltshire
and bound by Pegasus Bookbinding, Melksham, Wiltshire

CONTENTS

Claudian deserves more attention than is generally paid to him.

(S.T. Coleridge, *Table Talk*, August 18, 1833)

INTRODUCTION

1. Claudian and his historical background

Claudius Claudianus, the latest representative of the classical tradition in Latin poetry, a fervent admirer of Rome and all that she anciently stood for, and, at a time when the old religion was in its death throes, an obdurate and unabashed pagan[1] in a Christian court, came to Italy in all probability in the year A.D. 394. He stands in the great tradition of Roman poets whose origins are to be sought beyond the shores of Italy. His own clear testimony points to Egypt as his native land and to Alexandria as his native city,[2] and his familiarity with the sights and scenes of Egypt tends to confirm this.[3] Greek, therefore, must have been his first language, though his mastery of Latin suggests an early acquaintance with that language and a thorough training in its literature. Greek would have been the language of his earliest compositions when he embarked on the profession of poet in Alexandria, and fragments of a Greek *Gigantomachia* have survived from this period. When, about 394, he appeared on the Italian scene and began composing epideictic pieces for important public occasions, he brought to his task a Latinity so pure and brilliant and a metrical technique of such refinement as to raise the presumption that he was already widely practised in the making of Latin verse.

In that year, 394, the emperor Theodosius left Constantinople and marched against the Frankish Arbogast, who two years previously, after the murder of Valentinian II in his palace at Vienne, had set up Eugenius as emperor of the West. The two sides met in the valley of the Frigidus (Vipacco, Wippach) in the eastern spur of the Julian Alps near Trieste, and with the aid of a wind that blew the enemy's missiles back in their faces, Theodosius defeated the usurpers and made his way to Mediolanum. The younger of his two sons, Honorius Augustus, was summoned from Constantinople and made the journey in company with

---

1. *Adv. pag.* 7.35, *paganus pervicacissimus*; Cameron, 189ff.
2. *Carm. min.* 19.3; 22.56f.
3. Birt, *introd.* pp.i ff., esp. p.v.

Serena, niece and adopted daughter of Theodosius and wife of Stilicho, *comes* and *magister utriusque militiae*.[4] His elder son, Arcadius Augustus, remained at Constantinople in the charge of Rufinus, *praefectus praetorio Orientis*.[5] Theodosius died at Mediolanum on 17 January 395, commending his sons to the fatherly care of Stilicho. Honorius thereafter was emperor of the West and Arcadius of the East, and the Empire was not united again under a single ruler until the days of Justinian.

This was the state of affairs during what were probably Claudian's earliest days in Italy. How or when he came there we cannot be absolutely sure: external evidence for his life is very scanty. There is a short biographical notice in the Suda and one or two brief chronicle entries. That of Prosper Tiro for the year 395 reads: *hoc tempore Claudianus poeta innotuit*.[6] The nature of his major poems did not lend itself to personal confidences, but the fact that they were composed for datable occasions or to commemorate historical events makes it possible to arrange most of his works in a chronological sequence from 394 to 404. Further evidence is offered by certain of the *carmina minora* like the letters to Probinus and Olybrius.[7] There are, in addition, elegiac prefaces prefixed to some of the major poems, which provide details of the date and circumstances of composition. The highly poetical mode of expression that Claudian employs in these passages is, however, often open to more than one interpretation and in some ways they pose as many problems as they solve.

A sure starting-point is the panegyric that Claudian delivered early in January 395, to celebrate the consulship of the two young Anicii, Probinus and Olybrius, sons of a famous Christian, senatorial family. In the poem, the Goddess Roma is shown winging her way to Theodosius, still battle-stained from the battle at the Frigidus, and soliciting the honour for her two young favourites. In the letter to Probinus, Claudian states:

> Romanos bibimus primum te consule fontes
> et Latiae cessit Graia Thalia togae.[8]

("When you were consul, I first drank of Rome's fountains and

4.   *VI Cons. Hon.* 88ff.
5.   Zosimus 4.57.4.
6.   *Chronica minora* ed. T. Mommsen, *M.G.H. auct. ant.* IX, Berlin 1892.
7.   *Carm. min.* 41 and 40.
8.   *Carm. min.* 41.12f.

the Greek Muse gave way to the toga of Latium.") It would require great self-confidence to be sure that this couplet admits of one meaning to the exclusion of all others. Birt (who reads *accessit*) thought that it refers to the poet's change of domicile.[9] Cameron is sure that it means "that up till then (395) his literary output had been exclusively in Greek",[10] "that his panegyric on Probinus and Olybrius was his very first Latin poem" (i.e. "the first Latin poem he had publicly recited").[11] J.B. Hall, with more reason, follows others in understanding the lines to mean, "I drank from Roman sources of inspiration", and "I ceased writing on Greek themes and began to compose for members of the Roman Senate".[12]

To have won the office of panegyrist on such an important public occasion (presumably through the commendation of a patron) it is reasonable to suppose a period of residence of at least some months in Rome during the preceding year. The allusion to the battle of the Frigidus must mean that it was composed during the last months of 394 for recitation in January 395.

In the event it was evidently a resounding success, and twelve months later Claudian could boast:

> me quoque Pieriis temptatum saepius antris
> audet magna suo mittere Roma deo.
> iam dominas aures, iam regia tecta meremur
> et chelys Augusto iudice nostra sonat.[13]

("Me too, often tested in the Pierian caves, great Rome dares to send to her god. Now I have won the emperor's ear, now I have won an entrance to the imperial palace, and Augustus is the judge of the strains of my lyre.") His meaning is clear and his pride pardonable. From Rome he moved to Mediolanum, the seat of the Western court, and there in January 396 he delivered a panegyric on the occasion of the inaugural ceremonies of Honorius' third consulship. He was to remain at Mediolanum for the next five years and for the rest of his life he stood in close proximity to the Emperor and to Stilicho.

It is not to be supposed that this newcomer from Egypt,

9.   Birt, *introd.* p.viii.
10.   *Loc.cit.* p.7.
11.   *Loc.cit.* p.458.
12.   Claudian, *De Raptu Proserpinae*, Cambridge, 1969, p.102.
13.   *III Cons. Hon. praef.* 15ff.

whatever the success of his previous public poem, would have been allowed an entirely free hand in the remarks he addressed to Honorius and, more importantly, to the distinguished assembly gathered for the occasion. He would certainly have been given a careful briefing and his final draft would have been scrutinised and approved by Stilicho as guardian of the young Augustus' interests. There is, therefore, nothing in this speech that might have run at all counter to Stilicho's wishes, and it is in this poem that we have the famous scene in which the dying Theodosius charges Stilicho with the care of his sons.[14]

The working relationship thus established between the professional poet and the real ruler of the West was evidently a happy one. From this time until his death (or a silence that has been interpreted as death) Claudian faithfully and ably discharged the duty of representing Stilicho's actions in the best possible light and of discrediting his enemies. He was early given status by means of a post in Stilicho's service as *tribunus* and *notarius*, but does not appear to have aspired to any higher honours.

Not long before the recital of the poem on Honorius' third consulship, Rufinus, the *praefectus praetorio Orientis*, was murdered on 27 November 395 by Eastern troops detached from Stilicho's command in an expedition to Greece. It was inevitable in the circumstances that Rufinus should have been suspicious of Stilicho's intentions, especially in view of the unique position the latter was in to claim responsibility for safeguarding the interests of Arcadius as well as of Honorius. The reason for the expedition was the movement of Alaric, chief of the federate Visigothics, from Thrace downwards towards Constantinople and then westwards towards Greece; but before Stilicho had a chance to engage Alaric, he was ordered to return the Eastern contingent and withdraw. The two books *In Rufinum* were composed between 396 and the summer of 397. A preface, added later to the second book, postdates Stilicho's abortive second expedition to Greece in the spring and summer of 397. The work is customarily referred to as an invective, but, while it does contain much vituperation of Rufinus, it seems to have more in common structurally with the short epic poems Claudian composed later than with the inverse

14. *III Cons. Hon.* 142ff.

form of the rhetorically constructed panegyric.[15]

When towards the end of this year Claudian was called on to compose the panegyric for Honorius' consulship of 398, his fourth, the relationship between East and West was under very severe strain. Eutropius[16] had put a decisive curb on Stilicho's pretensions to influence in the East by inducing the senate of Constantinople to declare him *hostis publicus* and by the sequestration of any property of his situated in the East. He also sought to arrive at an accommodation with the Goths by concluding a *foedus* which conferred on Alaric the rank of *magister militum per Illyricum* and enabled him to draw on the imperial arsenals for the arming of his followers, who, about this time, elevated him on a shield as King of the Visigoths.[17] To make matters worse a crisis developed in the autumn when Gildo, *comes et magister utriusque militiae per Africam*, defected from Rome, entered into negotiations with Constantinople with a view to transferring his allegiance to the East, and severely curtailed the shipment of corn to Italy.

The situation was grave. The relationship between the *partes Imperii* was strained to breaking point. In the *Panegyricus de Quarto Consulatu Honorii*, however, Claudian put the best face he could on things and, in order not to spoil the great day by striking a sour note, heavily underlined the *concordia fratrum*, reiterated Stilicho's claim to joint guardianship, and played down all the unpleasantness by giving only the most oblique and nameless references to the current crisis.[18]

Only weeks after the inauguration, Stilicho deemed it advisable to strengthen his position by marrying his daughter Maria to Honorius, and soon after the delivery of the panegyric the hardworking Claudian came up with a set of *Fescennina* and an *Epithalamium*. This was a busy time for Claudian and there was to be no respite. Hardly, we are told, had the strains of the wedding-hymn died away when he was obliged to compose an account of the war undertaken against Gildo, not by Stilicho, but by Gildo's own brother Mascezel. The *De Bello Gildonico* is very largely a collection of set speeches. The contestants never

15. W. Barr, 'Claudian's *In Rufinum*: An Invective?', *Papers of the Liverpool Latin Seminar Second Volume 1979*, ed. F. Cairns (=ARCA 3), pp.179ff.
16. See below, p.00.
17. *In Eutr.* 2,214ff.; *Bell. Get.* 541ff.; Jordanes *Get.* 146.
18. *IV Cons. Hon.* 104-109, 391-392, 436-438.

reach the point of crossing swords and the work ends with Mascezel's fleet putting in to the harbour of Cagliari in Sardinia. As it stands the *De Bello Gildonico* is manifestly incomplete (it is sometimes labelled Book 1) and the question arises, Is this all Claudian wrote of it, or was the remainder lost or suppressed?[19] It should be noted that the hero of the hour was Mascezel, not Stilicho, and that his success may have proved his undoing. We learn that he was drowned on his return when crossing a bridge in the company of Stilicho.[20]

When Rufinus was murdered in 395, his place had been taken by the eunuch Eutropius, *praepositus sacri cubiculi*, who took the steps outlined above to resist Stilicho's interference. His hold over the premier Augustus was absolute. Arcadius, as much of a nonentity as his brother, has been compared, in Gibbon's elegant phrase, "to one of those harmless and simple animals who scarcely feel that they are the property of their shepherd".[21] No friend to Rufinus, he had deftly foiled a match between his daughter and Arcadius, and married him off to a bride of his own choosing, Eudoxia, who later engineered his downfall.[22] Eutropius assumed a *magisterium militare* and as a reward for a possibly successful campaign against the Huns in Asia Minor, which he led in 398, demanded and received the consulship of 399. The idea of a eunuch enjoying an honour not as yet bestowed on Stilicho was a flagrant affront to the West. So much so that Stilicho forbade the name of Eutropius to be entered in the fasti,[23] with the result that some of the chroniclers filled the blank by regarding his colleague, Mallius Theodorus, as two men, Mallius *and* Theodorus. This colleague, an eminently respectable lawyer and Neoplatonist philosopher, shared with Honorius and Stilicho and the two Anicii the rare privilege of being hymned by Claudian, when he entered upon his consulship at Mediolanum in January 399.

In the course of this year a rising of the Ostrogoths took place in Phrygia. One eastern army sent against them, commanded by Leo, a creature of Eutropius and a wool-carder by

19. E.M. Olechowska, *Cl. Claudiani De Bello Gildonico*, Leiden, 1978, pp.5ff.; S. Döpp, *Zeitgeschichte in Dichtungen Claudians*, Wiesbaden, 1980, pp.135ff.
20. Zosimus 5.11.
21. Gibbon, ch. 32; Zosimus 5.12, ὁ δὲ κυριεύων Ἀρκαδίου καθάπερ βοσκήματος.
22. Zosimus 5.3.
23. *Manl. Theod.* 266f.

trade, was heavily defeated by Tribigild. Gainas, who led the other eastern force, then conspired with Tribigild to demand from Arcadius the dismissal of Eutropius. The plan was favoured by Eudoxia, the empress, who hated Eutropius. He was disgraced, exiled to Cyprus, then brought back to Constantinople and put to death. Claudian devoted to the eunuch-consul the two books *In Eutropium*, a work of blistering vituperation. It may be said that Claudian shows to better effect in the *In Rufinum* and the *In Eutropium* than in his panegyrics, which have a fulsome quality often difficult to reconcile with complete sincerity. The venom he directs against Eutropius is of the purest and in this poem he moves still further away from the text-book invective. The *In Eutropium* contains many reminiscences of Juvenal, more popular at this time than he had ever been in his own lifetime, and is more heavily indebted to him than to Menander Rhetor.

In 400, Stilicho at last attained the consulship and Claudian honoured the occasion with a panegyric in two books, recited at Mediolanum in the early days of the new year. He is the only one of Claudian's honorands to be dignified with two books and, as if that were not enough, a third was added to celebrate Stilicho's triumphant entry into Rome, in the second half of February. It will be clear from what has been said already that Stilicho had not been to date the most conspicuously successful of generals, even by Claudian's own accounts. All that notwithstanding, Claudian returns to the subject of the war with Gildo, and this time there can be no mistaking who the hero of the undertaking really ought to have been. The third book shows Claudian in unusually high spirits even for him. In the preface to Book III, Stilicho is Scipio:

> quo concidit alter
> Hannibal antiquo saevior Hannibale[24]

("conqueror of a second Hannibal more terrible than Hannibal of old"). If Stilicho is Scipio, then Claudian is his Ennius.[25] The same preface also gives us to understand that for the occasion Claudian returned to Rome:

---

24. *Stil. 3 praef.* 21f.
25. *Stil. 3 praef.* 11.

te mihi post quintos annorum, Roma, recursus
reddidit et votis iussit adesse suis[26]

("After five years Stilicho has given you back to me, Rome, and ordered me to be present for the fulfilment of her prayer"). The poet's unfeigned delight in the occasion is evident in the patent sincerity of his eulogy of Rome at III 130ff. His efforts did not go unrewarded. Probably later in the same year a statue of the poet was erected by the emperors in the Forum of Trajan, and the inscription is still extant:

[Cl.] Claudiani v.c.
[Cla]udio Claudiano v.c. tri-
[bu]no et notario inter ceteras
[de]centes artes prae[g]loriosissimo
[po]etarum, licet ad memoriam sem-
piternam carmina ab eodem
scripta sufficiant, adtamen
testimonii gratia ob indicii sui
[f]idem dd. nn. Arcadius et Honorius
[f]elicissimi ac doctissimi
imperatores senatu petente
statuam in foro divi Traiani
erigi collocarique iusserunt.
Eἰν ἐνὶ Βιργιλίοιο νόον καὶ μοῦσαν Ὁμήρου
Κλαυδιανὸν Ῥώμη καὶ βασιλῆς ἔθεσαν.[27]

("Claudius Claudianus, *vir clarissimus*. To Claudius Claudianus, *v.c.*, tribune and notary, amongst other becoming accomplishments most glorious of poets, though the poems he wrote are enough to preserve his memory for ever, yet in testimony of his discretion and loyalty our most happy and learned emperors, Arcadius and Honorius, at the request of the senate, ordered this statue to be set up and placed in the Forum of the Divine Trajan. *Rome and her Emperors set up this statue of Claudianus, who combines the intellect of a Virgil with the Muse of a Homer.*")

Between these events and the appearance of the next poem to which a date can be confidently assigned (the *De Bello Getico* of 402) it would seem that Claudian took a rest from the

26. *Stil.* 3 *praef.* 23f.
27. *C.I.L.* vi. 1710 = L. Moretti, *Inscriptiones Graecae Urbis Romae*, Fasc. 1, Rome, 1968, no. 63.

court and the unrelenting demands it made on his services. The preface to that poem unambiguously indicates a resumption of his poetic efforts after a break.[28] We know from one of the *carmina minora*, the *Epistola ad Serenam*,[29] that he made a visit to Africa, where with the assistance of a letter of recommendation from her, he wooed and won a bride, of whom or her fate we know nothing. The letter ends with the promise of a panegyric for Serena, which is probably the incomplete poem called *Laus Serenae*.[30]

During Claudian's absence from Italy, Alaric and his Visigoths were on the march again. In autumn 401 they left Illyricum and, while Stilicho was busy tackling an incursion of Alans and Vandals in Noricum and Raetia, they crossed the Julian Alps and marched on Mediolanum. Stilicho reinforced his troops with contingents hastily withdrawn from Scotland and the Rhine,[31] and, swelling his forces still further with the defeated Alans and Vandals now received into Western service as *foederati*,[32] forced Alaric to withdraw from Mediolanum, and defeated him on Easter Sunday, 402, at Pollentia. The siege was lifted and the fear that a victorious Alaric might have swooped on Rome, whose walls had been renewed to meet this contingency, receded. Stilicho was in possession of the Gothic camp which was full of women and children, among them Alaric's own wife and family. Fears for their safety led Alaric to agree to a pact with Stilicho, which allowed the Goths to leave Italy. The pact was speedily dishonoured and later in the year Stilicho engaged and defeated Alaric at Verona. Once again, in spite of the desperate state of the Goths, their numbers seriously depleted by casualties, desertions and sickness, Stilicho did not press his advantage and Alaric was once more allowed to live, to fight another day and eventually, eight years later, to enter Rome. It is small wonder that Orosius was moved to say: *taceo de Alarico . . . saepe victo, saepe concluso, semperque dimisso* ("I say nothing of Alaric, often defeated, often hemmed in and regularly allowed to escape").[33] It is hard to

28. *Bell. Get. praef.* 1, *post resides annos longo velut excita somno/Romanis fruitur nostra Thalia choris.*
29. *Carm. min.* 31.55f.
30. *Carm. min.* 30.
31. *Bell. Get.* 416f.
32. *Bell. Get.* 581ff.
33. *Adv. pag.* 7.57.1.

know why Stilicho should not have crushed Alaric once and for all when he had it in his power. One explanation is that his failure to do so represents a continuation of Theodosius' policy of clemency.[34]

Claudian commemorated Stilicho's victory in the *De Bello Getico*, written soon after Pollentia and before Verona. The work, as befits the occasion, is high-spirited and contains a pleasant enough little piece of nonsense concerning an oracle given to Alaric:

Rumpe omnes, Alarice, moras; hoc impiger annO
Alpibus Italiae ruptis penetrabis ad UrbeM[35]

("Brook no delay, Alaric; break vigorously through the Alps and you will reach the city"). Those who have a mind to, may care to discover just how many times the letters ROMA are contained in these two lines.[36] Like all oracles it was deceitful and the Urbs was not Rome but an insignificant river. One tiny and endearing detail in the poem does more perhaps to make Stilicho come alive for the reader than all else that Claudian has written about him: the joy of the beleaguered citizens of Mediolanum when they saw a white-headed man leading the army that was marching to their relief and knew that this was Stilicho.[37]

With Alaric still on the loose, Mediolanum was now considered too dangerous to house the court and so Honorius moved to Ravenna. From here in 403 he emerged to enter Rome in triumph for the recent victory and returned again at the beginning of 404 for the inaugural ceremonies of his sixth consulship. With his *Panegyricus de Sexto Consulatu Honorii* the long series of Claudian's datable compositions comes to a halt. Coupled as it was with the now rare occurrence of an imperial visit to Rome, the occasion was one of more than ordinary significance. Claudian omits some of the structural divisions of panegyric, and devotes much of the poem to Alaric's two defeats, with some not wholly convincing explanations of Stilicho's policy in regard to the fact of his being allowed to survive. There follows Rome's plea to Honorius to

34. E. Stein, *Histoire du Bas-Empire*, Bruges, 1959, I (1) p.249; see note on *IV Cons. Hon.* 113.
35. *Bell. Get.* 546f.
36. See note on *IV Cons. Hon.* 644ff.
37. *Bell. Get.* 457ff.

visit her, and his speech of assent, an account of the journey from Ravenna, a description of the city with its new walls (decked out like a girl by her anxious mother when a suitor is expected), and the poem ends with the games in the circus.

It used to be assumed that Claudian was involved in Stilicho's downfall and perished with him in 408, but it is difficult on that theory to explain why in the four years that preceded this there should have been nothing from his pen to commemorate Stilicho's consulship of 405, or, more significantly even, his silence regarding the very real success of Stilicho at Faesulae in 406 over a huge barbarian horde that invaded Italy under Radagaisus. All things considered, it seems safest to assume that Claudian's death must have occurred in 404.

One major poem in three books stands outside the canon of Claudian's work described above. This is the incomplete mythological epic *De Raptu Proserpinae*, with its puzzling preface dedicatory to Florentinus heading the second book. There are grounds for thinking that the first book may have been written at an early date in Claudian's career and books two and three added after a break of some years, but exactly when it would be difficult to say with certainty.[38]

The fact that those poems which concern Stilicho have been transmitted separately from the rest of Claudian's work raises the presumption that they were collected and edited at Stilicho's direction soon after the poet's death. The *carmina minora* were added to these and from as early as the fifth century transmitted together with the major group of Stilichonian poems to form the corpus called *Claudianus maior*. The Panegyric for Probinus and Olybrius has been transmitted independently of *Claudianus maior*, as was the *De Raptu Proserpinae*, or *Claudianus minor*.

2.   The Latin Panegyric

While encomiastic elements may be found in virtually any kind of literary genre, from epic to political and forensic speeches, the earliest examples of the Latin panegyric are afforded by the *laudationes funebres*, the funeral speeches that

38. See Hall, *loc.cit.* pp.93ff.

formed part of the rites of the patrician *gentes*.[39] Praise of living heroes is as natural a phenomenon as praise of the dead and begins to occur at an early stage of Rome's literary history. In this connection one thinks of Ennius and the services he performed for M. Fulvius Nobilior in the *Annales*, and for Scipio Africanus in the poem *Scipio* that celebrated his exploits. It is not without significance that Claudian should have worked out his preface to the third book of the praise of Stilicho in terms of Scipio and Ennius. In Lucilius we note the advice offered at 621M:

> percrepa pugnam Popili, facta Corneli cane,

a sure way of obtaining praise and profit (620M). This, in turn, reminds us of the advice Trebatius Testa gives to Horace:

> aude
> Caesaris invicti res dicere, multa laborum
> praemia laturus.[40]

Whether the literary productions envisaged in these passages are epic or panegyric is hard to say, but at all events the panegyric had certainly emerged by now as a separate form, and the scholiast on Horace, *Epist.* 1.16.27 marks the verse as *Varii in panegyrico Augusti*. Still extant are a *Panegyricus Messallae*, attached to the *Corpus Tibullianum* in 212 hexameters, and composed between 31 and 27 B.C., and a *Laus Pisonis* in 261 hexameters, belonging to the Neronian age.

The imperial age saw the rise of the *gratiarum actio* in which newly elected consuls returned thanks publicly for the honour conferred on them and it is from this kind of speech, heavily charged with praise of the emperor, that consular panegyrics like those of Claudian and his imitator Sidonius Apollinaris (5th cent.), pronounced now by someone other than the new consul, developed. The earliest extant *gratiarum actio* is that of Pliny the Younger, thanking Trajan for his elevation to the consulship in A.D. 100. Pliny's *Panegyricus*, as it is called, heads the collection called *XII Panegyrici Latini*,[41] which contains, as well as Mamertinus' *gratiarum actio* to Julian giving thanks for his consulship, other similar speeches delivered on

---

39. F. Vollmer, *Laudationum funebrium Romanorum historiae et reliquiarum editio*, Leipsig, 1891.
40. Hor. *Serm.* 2.1.10ff.
41. Ed. R.A.B. Mynors, Oxford, 1964.

important public occasions. Of particular interest in this collection is the *Panegyricus Latini Pacati Drepani dictus Theodosio*, delivered before Theodosius at Rome on the occasion of his victory over Maximus. It was, as will be evident from the commentary, well known to Claudian and in the forefront of his mind when he composed his panegyric on Honorius' fourth consulship.

Q. Aurelius Symmachus,[42] one of the leaders of the pagan aristocracy in our period, was the author of prose panegyrics, the earliest of which was delivered at the quinquennial festival of 369, in honour of Valentinian I. His panegyric for Gratian was probably delivered about the same time.[43] Symmachus also celebrated Valentinian's third consulship in 370 and the second consulship of the pretender Maximus in 388. The first three orations we possess almost in their entirety. We know of the fourth from the ecclesiastical historian Socrates, who tells us that it caused Symmachus to be impeached for treason and that he was pardoned by Theodosius after seeking refuge in a church.[44] Also close in point of time to Claudian's consular panegyrics is the *gratiarum actio* delivered by Ausonius in 379, praising Gratian and thanking him for the honour of the consulship.[45]

Those orations mentioned above which formed part of the ceremonies marking the inauguration of a consul are prose works. One of Claudian's major contributions to the genre is to have established verse as the medium for this kind of composition, and in this he was followed by Sidonius Apollinaris and Corippus (6th cent.).[46] Some mention, however, should be made of Statius, *Silv.* 4.1, in which the poet congratulates Domitian on the occasion of his seventeenth consulship. This is a poem consisting of a mere 47 hexameters, which in scale and extent cannot be compared with even the shortest of Claudian's consular panegyrics or with the prose works mentioned above. Nevertheless, the topoi employed by Statius are very substantially the same as those which Claudian uses, particularly in the proem and epilogue. The opening lines of Statius' poem deal

---

42. Ed. O. Seeck, *M.G.H. auct. ant.* VI, Berlin, 1883.
43. Seeck, p.ccx.
44. Socrates 5.14.
45. Ed. K. Schenkl, *M.G.H. auct. ant.* V, Berlin, 1883.
46. Ennodius (473-521), ed. F. Vogel, *M.G.H. auct. ant.* VII, Berlin, 1885, reverted to prose for his panegyric on Theoderic.

with the trappings and ceremonial attached to the consulship — the purple, the curule chair, the lictors and axes. As usual, the imperial consulship ushers in no ordinary year but an *insignis annus*. The god Janus addresses the emperor at length and his speech forms the bulk of the poem. Claudian, too, shows a marked propensity for introducing a divinity, regularly the personified figure of Roma, to address his honorands.[47] Statius notes an unusual splendour about everything and even the winter is noticeably warmer. There is a comparison with Augustus and his many consulships, and the poem ends by reminding the new consul of the nations still to be conquered, in much the same way that Claudian ends the panegyrics on the third and fourth consulships of Honorius. What is particularly striking is that both the beginning and the end of *IV Cons. Hon.* contain echoes of this poem of Statius.[48] It is difficult to know whether in fact this poem formed part of the inaugural ceremonies, or was merely one of Statius' occasional poems of congratulation,[49] but at all events, prose seems to have remained the accepted medium for consular panegyrics until the time of Claudian.

3. The Panegyric on the IVth Consulate of Honorius

This is the third of the panegyrics written by Claudian after his arrival in Italy and, to date, the longest, over three times longer than the poem written for the third consulship just two years previously. His task was made no easier by the fact that in the interval between the two poems the young Augustus had achieved nothing more noteworthy than the celebration of his thirteenth birthday. Relations between East and West were strained to their limits. Silicho was a *hostis publicus* in the eyes of Constantinople. Gildo's revolt in Africa was causing a severe shortage of corn. Altogether the prospect in the Western part of the empire was about as depressing as it could possibly be. In the circumstances the poem that Claudian contrived for the occasion emerges as a masterpiece of ingenuity and tact. The rules of the genre imposed a general overall structure for the panegyric and within each section there were several customary

47. Cf. Cameron, *loc.cit.* pp.254f.
48. See notes on *IV Cons. Hon.* 2, *iactantior*; 653, *Babylonis*; and 656, *Bactra*.
49. The preface to Book 4 of the *Silvae* merely says, *primo autem septimum decimum Germanici nostri consulatum.*

topoi to be treated. Claudian's skill as an encomiast shows to good advantage in this poem in the way that he manipulates his subject-matter, some of which had inevitably been deployed in the earlier panegyric on Honorius, while conforming closely to the general principles laid down for the genre.

The patterns suggested for the panegyric by Aphthonius[50] and Menander[51] are very similar. These are προοίμιον (introduction), γένος (family), γένεσις (circumstances of birth and attendant omens), ἀνατροφή (upbringing), ἐπιτηδεύματα (pursuits and inclinations as evidence of character), πράξεις (exploits in war and peace so arranged as to illustrate the cardinal virtues), συγκρίσεις (comparisons), ἐπίλογος (conclusion with prayers and good wishes). On the whole, as will be seen from the running analysis supplied in the commentary, Claudian complies very closely with this pattern, except in the matter of συγκρίσεις, which he tends to disperse throughout the work instead of making a separate section.

In the earlier poem on Honorius, he virtually omitted the γένος section, contenting himself with a few lines on the exploits of Theodosius the elder (52-58), which he worked into the section on ἀνατροφή. His account of the emperor Theodosius was postponed to the πράξεις section, and used there to compensate for the lack of achievement of his main subject, Honorius. This is done by the clever device of attributing Theodosius' victories to the auspices of Honorius:

> pugnastis uterque:
> tu fatis genitorque manu.[52]

Claudian's sparing use of this material in the earlier poem left him free to develop the γένος section more fully in *IV Cons. Hon.*, and, when he was obliged to praise Honorius a third time, he was not under the necessity of repeating the same material. This he might easily have done, since one of his greatest gifts is the ability to produce the same thoughts again and again, diversified only by elegant variations of language; but, in fact, the γένος section of *VI Cons. Hon.* amounts to a mere 40 lines (25-64). *IV Cons. Hon.* contains the fullest development of the immediate forebears of Honorius (18-121) and their exploits,

---

50. *Rhetores Graeci*, ed. L. Spengel, vol. 2, Leipsig, 1854.
51. *Ibid.* vol. 3, Leipsig, 1856.
52. *III Cons. Hon.* 88f.

and the emphasis laid on Theodosius the elder's African campaign and his son's defeat of the two pretenders must have held a tacit promise of a like fate awaiting Gildo.

The most striking feature of this poem is, however, the unusual amount of space devoted to upbringing and education (ἀνατροφή) — considerably more than one-third of the whole poem (159-427), as compared with a mere 41 lines in *III Cons. Hon.* (22-62) and a total disregard of the subject in *VI Cons. Hon.* At this point Claudian cleverly and appropriately inserts a *speculum principis* or discourse on kingship of the kind that Synesius was later to pronounce before Honorius' brother Arcadius at Constantinople.[53] This is presented in the form of fatherly advice delivered by Theodosius to his son in the form of a speech (214-418), interrupted by a plea from Honorius to be allowed to put these precepts into practice and follow his father into battle (352-369). This interruption serves the purpose of an ἐπιτηδεύματα section and its insertion into the ἀνατροφή section affords further confirmation of Claudian's refusal to be shackled by rhetorical instruction while by no means ignoring it. The impatient outburst of Honorius also has the effect of usefully shattering the tedium of a long, didactic discourse. In *IV Cons. Hon.* two distinct genres are welded together in an ingenious way — the panegyric and the *speculum principis*. The tender age of Honorius and the hopes that at this period might justifiably have been entertained for him make Claudian's procedure entirely appropriate and well suited to the occasion, and, certainly so far as this particular panegyric is concerned (or indeed any of the other panegyrics of Claudian, laden as they are with political overtones), it is difficult to agree with Oswyn Murray that "ultimately the ceremonial aspect may be the most important".[54] The paraenetic function of these compositions is stressed by Pliny in his *Panegyricus*: *ut . . . boni principes quae facerent recognoscerent, mali quae facere deberent.*[55]

Unfortunately for the Roman world, Claudian's eloquent precepts, so tactfully represented as emanating from the mouth

---

53. See notes on 214-218.
54. Review of J.A. Straub, *Vom Herrscherideal in der Spätantike*, Stuttgart, 1964, in *Classical Review* N.S. 16, 1966, p.105.
55. 4.1. Cf. also Pliny *Epist.* 3.18.2, and on the whole subject Döpp, *loc.cit.* pp.18f., with the literature there cited.

of Theodosius himself, were wasted on their addressee. He was doomed to be one of history's great nonentities and to have his memory saddled with the story that, when Alaric sacked Rome in 410, he was feeding his poultry in Ravenna.[56] Despite the singularly unpromising nature of his subject, Claudian's πράξεις section runs to nearly two hundred lines (428-618). This is largely achieved by a similar ruse to that which he employed in *III Cons. Hon.*, where Theodosius' successes were attributed to Honorius' auspices. In *IV Cons. Hon.* much of the πράξεις section is filled up with accounts of Stilicho's recruiting campaign along the Rhine in 396 and his abortive expedition to Greece in 397 (439-487). Neatly (if implausibly) Claudian represents Stilicho as undertaking these campaigns under Honorius' express orders and with his approval.[57] The remainder of the section is devoted to Honorius' beauty, strength and horsemanship, and to a further account of his arrival in Mediolanum in 394. This Claudian had already described in *III Cons. Hon.*, where the journey that preceded it is elevated almost to an undertaking of high adventure.[58] Claudian's love of ecphrasis appears in the elaborate description of Honorius' robes — a description that does little credit to the taste of either the encomiast or the wearer. The speech ends with the usual prayers and high hopes for the future, in much the same way as *III Cons. Hon.*

All in all, this panegyric affords a good example of Claudian's skill in this branch of his art, though in one respect he does not avail himself of a favourite device of his. This is the personification of peoples, cities and abstract qualities (Roma, Iustitia, etc.), which are regularly introduced for the purpose of delivering a major speech. The *Bellum Gildonicum* is a good example of this technique. Most probably Claudian felt that the weight of Theodosius' discourse on kingship was as much as the poem could stand in the way of speeches without introducing others. It was, however, on this single speech that the fame of *IV Cons. Hon.* later rested. It became a rich quarry for the compilers of medieval *florilegia*, and was widely quoted by, for example, John of Salisbury, both in the *Polycraticon* and

---

56. Procopius *Hist. Bell.* 3.2.25.
57. *iubes*, 440; *hortaris*, 460.
58. *III Cons. Hon.* 111ff.

in the *Vita S. Anselmi*, and by Vincent of Beauvais in his
Speculum Docrinale.[59]

4.   Claudian's metrical technique

For one whose mother tongue was not Latin Claudian's
prosody can scarcely be faulted and his admirers have tended to
point with pride to his "one false quantity": *ferĭtura* (*Rapt.
Pros.* 3,359), which J.B. Hall eliminates by accepting J.J.
Scaliger's conjecture *petit ira* into his text.[60] To *feritura* may be
added *flumen Acim* (*Rapt. Pros.* 3.332) of all the extant mss.,
for which Hall substitutes *flavum Acin*, reported by Claverius
from an otherwise unknown codex,[61] and *Syphācem* at *Bell.
Gild.* 91.[62]

The qualities of Claudian's verse most likely to strike the
reader, however, are its exceptional smoothness and regularity,
qualities which are achieved by the avoidance of elision and
prosodic licence, and by the constantly recurring use of hexameters of similar construction. If these qualities give his verse
some claim to flawless perfection, equally it must be said they
rob it of variety and give rise to the charge of monotony so
often levelled against it.

Of the sixteen possible combinations of dactyls and spon-
dees in the first four feet of a hexameter, Duckworth[63] shows
that Claudian's favourite types of verse are, in order of frequency:

DSDS
DSSS
SDSS
DDSS
SSDS
DDDS
SDDS
DSSD

His calculation, based on *In Eutr.* 1 and 2, *III Cons. Hon.* and
IV Cons. Hon., shows that these eight schemes alone account

59. Birt, ch. vii, *de excerptorum codicibus*.
60. Hall, *loc.cit.*, p.179 and p.240.
61. Hall, p.177 and p.233.
62. Olechowska, *loc.cit.* p.23 and p.150.
63. G.E. Duckworth, 'Five Centures of Latin Hexameter Poetry: Silver Age and
Late Empire', *Transactions and Proceedings of the American Philological
Association*, 98, 1967, pp.77ff.

for 82.21% of the whole. *IV Cons. Hon.* runs entirely true to Duckworth's conclusion, yielding a total of 83.23% for these eight types. The application of Duckworth's concept of "repeat clusters" (i.e. passages in which the same metrical pattern appears six or more times in a unit of sixteen lines or fewer) as a test of metrical monotony, shows that this phenomenon occurs once in every 67.8 lines of the poems examined. The corresponding figure for Virgil is once in 200.1 verses, for Statius *Thebaid* once in 101.1, and for Valerius Flaccus once in 44.7 verses.

The end of the line is regularly constructed. There are no monosyllabic endings or *spondeiazontes* in this poem, and only once does Claudian end the line with a word of four syllables, *armipotens Lacedaemon* (508), and that, as in his five other examples, is a Greek word.[64] Here again, however, we find the same type of ending being used several times in succession – a practice that again makes for monotony. Thus in *IV Cons. Hon.* the type *lenibus ulnis* occurs four times in succession (167-170), followed at once by the type *praesentior aether* thrice repeated (171-173). The first type occurs five times in succession at 325-329. In 360-363, a further type, *praedonis acerbi*, occurs four times in sequence, followed immediately by a run of the type *da protinus arma* (363-365). Verses 642-645 again repeat the same type of ending (*gaudia mundo*).

Claudian tends to break his hexameter with caesuras at three points in the line, second, third and fourth feet, and especially noteworthy is the high incidence of third trochee caesura. In *IV Cons. Hon.* verses of these types occur with the following frequency:

auspiciis | iterum || sese | regalibus annus   160=24.4%
iam trabeam | Bellona || gerit | parmamque removit 152=23.2%

The effect of this high incidence of third trochee caesura is to curtail the interplay of ictus and accent at this part of the verse and in this respect Claudian is following post-Augustan practice.[65]

The feature of Claudian's verse most commonly remarked

64. Birt, p.ccxv.
65. Birt, p.ccxii: *exaggerat etiam consuetudinem Statii et paene Valerium Flaccum aequiparat apud quem maxima fere in litteris latinis eius formae frequentia est.*

on is his sparing use of elision, which he avoids to an extent unprecedented in Latin verse. *IV Cons. Hon.* shows 18 examples in 656 verses, of which all but two (*Garganum Alpinis*, 106, and *mandatricem operis*, 236) involve short final syllable. The incidence of elision in this poem is, therefore, 2.7%[66] as compared with 10 elisions in 211 lines, or 4.7%, in *III Cons. Hon.* and 18 elisions in 526 lines, or 3.4%, in *Bell. Gild.*[67] A rough count of my own for ten of the poems in the *Claudianus maior* yields a figure of 1 elision per 21 lines, or 4.8%. This compares with Virgil *Aen.* 54.4%, Lucan 11.8%, Valerius Flaccus 28.3% and Statius *Theb.* 1 39%.[68] It will be seen that in the matter of elision Claudian is something of an individualist, nor is his practice in this respect consistent. The low incidence of elision in *Rapt. Pros.* 1, 1.7%, is unusual even for him,[69] and *In Ruf.* and *VI Cons. Hon.*, according to my count, show a higher than average incidence with 6.1% and 6.7% respectively. Within the 656 lines of *IV Cons. Hon.* there is an uneven distribution of elision, the bulk occurring in the first half of the poem for no immediately obvious reason.

Smooth, elegant and correct Claudian's verses certainly are, but their very excellence in these respects undeniably produces a certain tedium and it is difficult, however much one may applaud his achievement, not to sympathise with one critic who remarked that "his graces are often of the engine-turned quality and his lustre metallic".[70]

5.   Text

The text here offered makes no claim to be based on a fresh study of the manuscripts and the variant readings noted are as reported in Birt's apparatus. Students of the textual criticism of Claudian have found cause to complain of Birt's excessive adherence to a handful of chosen witnesses[71] and, in

---

66. Hall's figure of 1 elision per 46.8 lines for this poem would appear to be incorrect (p.110 n.4).
67. Olechowska, *loc.cit.* p.22.
68. These figures are taken from the compilation in D. Güntzschel, *Beiträge zur Datierung des Culex*, Münster, 1972, p.40. See also J. Soubiran, *L'Elision dans la Poésie Latine*, Paris, 1966.
69. Hall, *loc.cit.* p.110 n.4.
70. J.P. Postgate in his review of the editions of Birt and Koch, *Classical Review*, 9, 1895, pp.162ff.
71. Hall, *loc.cit.* p.91. His criticism is as valid for *Claudianus maior* as for *Claudianus minor*.

his description of his groups of witnesses, of a classification that is inexact and insufficiently justified.[72] His text, and indeed the whole body of his work on Claudian, however, makes a considerable advance on anything previously available, and despite its conservatism will remain indispensable until *Claudianus maior* is re-edited on the same excellent principles as Hall's *De Raptu Proserpinae*. The present text differs from Birt at only a few points.

Birt constructed his text of *Claudianus maior* on the basis of seven mss., of which six are of the first rank and the seventh he classes among the *deteriores*. Of these only the following need be mentioned for present purposes: two of Birt's basic mss. do not contain *IV Cons. Hon.*:[73]

P   Parisiensis Bibl. Nat. Lat. 18552 membr. 8°. 12-13 cent. (Birt, p.xcv)

Π   Parisiensis Bibl. Nat. Lat. 8082 membr. 8°. 13 cent. (Birt, p.xcvii)

B   Codex Neapolitanus Borbonicus (Farnesianus) IIII E. 47 membr. 8°. 13 cent. (Birt, p.xcvii)

A   Mediolanensis Ambrosianus S.66 sup., membr. 4°. 15 cent. (Birt, p.xcvii)

Also referred to are the readings of non-extant mss. preserved in the interlineations and marginalia of the *editio princeps* and other early printed editions. These are:

E and Em   The *Excerpta Florentina*. These appear in a copy of
Λ   the *editio princeps* or *editio Vincentina* (Λ) (Barnabus Celsanus, Vicenza, 1482). The writer of these *excerpta* used two mss., a *Codex Lucensis* and one he calls *antiquus b*. They are called E when they are interlinear, Em when they are marginal.
          (Birt, pp.lxxxii ff.)

ε   The *Excerpta Gyraldina*. Corrections in a copy of the *editio Aldina* (F. Asulanus, Venice, 1523) by Gregorius Giraldus *ex vetustissimo exemplari sumpto ab Aenea*

---

72. Olechowska, *loc.cit.* p.55.
73. These are *Codex Vaticanus* 2809 (V) and *Codex Bruxellensis* 5380-4 (C).

Gerardino, closely resembling E and Em.
(Birt, pp.lxxxv ff.)

Isengr. mg.   Unlike E, Em and ϵ, these are printed, not written, in the margin of the edition of M. Bentinus (M. Isengrinius, Basle, 1534), from a lost *Codex Capitonis*. This edition is of particular importance for *IV Cons. Hon.*, especially in view of the absence of this poem from *Codex Vaticanus* 2809, and contains some verses found in no other ms.
(Birt, pp.clxxxvii)

dett.   For the *codices deteriores* occasionally referred to, see Birt pp.cxviii ff.

codd.   The consensus of the mss.

Acknowledgements

My gratitude is due to Sandra Cairns, Jonathan Foster and Duncan Kennedy for their academic advice upon this volume and for their assistance with proof-reading.

TEXT

TRANSLATION

PANEGYRICUS
DE QUARTO CONSULATU
HONORII AUGUSTI

Auspiciis iterum sese regalibus annus
induit et nota fruitur iactantior aula;
limina nec passi circum privata morari
exultant reduces Augusto consule fasces.
cernis ut armorum proceres legumque potentes   5
patricios sumunt habitus et more Gabino
discolor incedit legio positisque parumper
bellorum signis sequitur vexilla Quirini?
lictori cedunt aquilae ridetque togatus
miles et in mediis effulget curia castris.   10
ipsa Palatino circumvallata senatu
iam trabeam Bellona gerit parmamque removit
et galeam sacras umeris vectura curules.
nec te laurigeras pudeat, Gradive, secures
pacata gestare manu Latiaque micantem   15
loricam mutare toga, dum ferreus haeret
currus et Eridani ludunt per prata iugales.
     Haud indigna coli nec nuper cognita Marti
Ulpia progenies et, quae diademata mundo
sparsit, Hibera domus. nec tantam vilior unda   20
promeruit gentis seriem: cunabula fovit
Oceanus: terrae dominos pelagique futuros
inmenso decuit rerum de principe nasci.
hinc processit avus, cui post Arctoa frementi
classica Massylas adnexuit Africa laurus,   25
ille, Caledoniis posuit qui castra pruinis,
qui medios Libyae sub casside pertulit aestus,
terribilis Mauro debellatorque Britanni
litoris ac pariter Boreae vastator et Austri.

14 *versus deest in* ΡΑΠ, *exstat in* ΒΛ.

PANEGYRIC
ON THE FOURTH CONSULATE
OF THE EMPEROR HONORIUS

Once again the auspices the year assumes are royal, and prouder now, it rejoices in the familiar palace; the returning fasces, disdaining to linger around the thresholds of commoners, exult in the consulship of Augustus. Do you see how the lords of war and the great law-makers put on the garb of senators, and how the legion marches in sober array, wearing the Gabine fold, and follows the banners of Quirinus, their standards of war put by for a while? The eagles give way to the lictor, the toga-clad soldiery smile and the senate-house shines in the midst of the camp. Bellona herself, surrounded by the Palatine council, wears a consular gown and has taken off her shield and helmet to bear on her shoulders the sacred curule-chair. Be not ashamed, Gradivus, to carry the laurel-decked axes in a peaceful hand and exchange the shining breastplate for a Latian toga, while your iron chariot stands fast and its team plays on the meadows of Eridanus.

The line of Trajan and its Spanish home that has scattered crowns over the earth is not undeserving to be honoured, nor newly acquainted with Mars. No lesser stream won for itself the great honour of this dynasty: Ocean it was that tended its cradle: the future lords of earth and sea are rightly descended from the measureless originator of all things. Hence came your grandfather, on whom, still in battle-cry after his northern campaigns, Africa pinned laurels won from the Massyli, he who pitched camp on the Caledonian frosts, who bore the midday heat of Libya upon his helmet, terrible to the Moor, conqueror of the British shore, and ravager of North and South alike.

quid rigor aeternus caeli, quid frigora prosunt   30
ignotumque fretum? maduerunt Saxone fuso
Orcades; incaluit Pictorum sanguine Thyle;
Scottorum cumulos flevit glacialis Hiberne.
quid calor obsistit forti? per vasta cucurrit
Aethiopum cinxitque novis Atlanta maniplis;   35
virgineum Tritona bibit sparsosque venenis
Gorgoneos vidit thalamos et vile virentes
Hesperidum risit, quos ditat fabula, ramos.
arx incensa Iubae, rabies Maurusia ferro
cessit et antiqui penetralia diruta Bocchi.   40
    Sed laudes genitor longe transgressus avitas
subdidit Oceanum sceptris et margine caeli
clausit opes, quantum distant a Tigride Gades,
inter se Tanais quantum Nilusque relinquunt:
haec tamen innumeris per se quaesita trophaeis   45
non generis dono, non ambitione potitus.
digna legi virtus: ultro se purpura supplex
obtulit et solus meruit regnare rogatus.
nam, cum barbaries penitus commota gementem
inrueret Rhodopen et mixto turbine gentes   50
iam deserta suas in nos transfunderet Arctos,
Danubii totae vomerent cum proelia ripae,
cum Geticis ingens premeretur Mysia plaustris
flavaque Bistonios operirent agmina campos,
omnibus adflictis et vel labentibus ictu   55
vel prope casuris, unus tot funera contra
restitit extinxitque faces agrisque colonos
reddidit et leti rapuit de faucibus urbes.
nulla relicta foret Romani nominis umbra,
ni pater ille tuus iamiam ruitura subisset   60
pondera turbatamque ratem certaque levasset
naufragium commune manu: velut ordine rupto
cum procul insanae traherent Phaethonta quadrigae
saeviretque dies terramque et stagna propinqui

30 frigora: sidera B.   31 Saxone: sanguine Π^2B.   32 hiberne PΠB, hyberne
A, hibernae Λ (cf. Stil. 2.251, hibernam PΠB), Ierne, Hiverne, Iuverne,
editores. 46 potitus ΠA, potitur EmPB. 57 agrisque colonos: PAΠ, agrique
colonos ϵ, agrosque colonis BΛ.

What protection are unremitting harshness of climate, the cold, the uncharted sea against him? The Orkneys weltered in carnage wreaked on the Saxons; Thule grew warm with the blood of the Picts; icy Hibernia melted in tears over the mounds of the Scots. Does heat prevail at all against the hero? He overran the waste-places of Ethiopia and circled Atlas with troops new to those parts; he drank of Triton, Pallas' lake, saw the poison-spattered dens of the Gorgons, and laughed to find the branches of the Hesperides green and common after all, though legend makes them gold. He fired the citadel of Juba, the madness of the Moors gave way before his sword, and the fortress of old Bocchus was destroyed.

But your father far outstripped the praises of your grand-father, brought Ocean under his sway and set the rim of heaven as limit to his empire, from the Tigris to Cadiz and all that lies between the Nile and the Tanais: yet these he won by his own hand in countless victories, gained not by gift of birth nor for his asking. His merit justified the choice: of its own accord the suppliant purple offered itself and he alone, when asked, deserved to rule. For when Barbary, stirred to its depths, rushed upon troubled Rhodope and the North, now deserted, poured its peoples in a turmoil of confusion upon us, when the Danube all along its banks vomited battles, when huge Mysia felt the weight of Gothic wagons and the yellow-headed hordes covered the fields of Thrace, when all were stricken and either reeling from the blow or on the point of falling, one man with-stood so many disasters, extinguished the flames, restored the farmers to their fields and snatched cities from the jaws of death. No shadow of the Roman name would have survived, had not that father of yours shored up the falling mass on the point of collapse, steadied the ship in its distress, and with sure hand staved off the shipwreck threatening all: just as, when in broken order the maddened chariot-team was dragging Phaethon far off course, and the day's heat was raging, and the solar rays in their nearness were drinking up earth and its lakes,

haurirent radii, solito cum murmure torvis   65
sol occurrit equis; qui postquam rursus eriles
agnovere sonos, rediit meliore magistro
machina concentusque poli, currusque recepit
imperium flammaeque modum. sic traditus illi
servatusque Oriens. at non pars altera rerum   70
tradita: bis possessa manu, bis parta periclis.
per varium gemini scelus erupere tyranni
tractibus occiduis: hunc saeva Britannia fudit;
hunc sibi Germanus famulum delegerat exul:
ausus uterque nefas, domini respersus uterque   75
insontis iugulo. novitas audere priori
suadebat cautumque dabant exempla sequentem.
hic nova moliri praeceps, hic quaerere tuta
providus; hic fusis, collectis viribus ille;
hic vagus excurrens, hic intra claustra reductus.   80
dissimiles, sed morte pares. evadere neutri
dedecus aut mixtis licuit procumbere telis.
amissa specie, raptis insignibus ambo
in vultus rediere suos manibusque revinctis
oblati gladiis summittunt colla paratis   85
et vitam veniamque rogant. pro damna pudoris!
qui modo tam densas nutu movere cohortes,
in quos iam dubius sese libraverat orbis,
non hostes victore cadunt, sed iudice sontes:
damnat voce reos, petiit quos Marte tyrannos.   90
amborum periere duces; hic sponte carina
decidit in fluctus, illum suus abstulit ensis;
hunc Alpes, hunc pontus habet. solacia caesis
fratribus haec ultor tribuit: necis auctor uterque
labitur; Augustas par victima mitigat umbras.   95
has dedit inferias tumulis, iuvenumque duorum
purpureos merito placavit sanguine manes.
　　Illi iustitiam confirmavere triumphi,
praesentes docuere deos. hinc saecula discant

68 currus ε Isengr. mg., cursus P1, rursus P2 cett.   77 cautum Em, tantum
cett.

with his familiar soft voice the Sun came up to his savage horses; and when they recognised once more their master's accents, heavenly order and harmony were restored under a better ruler, the chariot again accepted his command, and the flames their proper limits. Thus was the East entrusted to him, thus preserved. Not so earth's other half: twice it was secured by his efforts, twice won by his perils. In the regions of the West, through different kinds of rascality, two tyrants emerged: savage Britain spawned one, a German exile chose the other to do his bidding; both attempted unspeakable crime, both were spattered by the blood of a guiltless emperor. Insolence prompted the first to boldness, and his example made the second wary. One was hasty in stirring up rebellion, the other shrewd in seeking safe counsel; one deployed, the other contracted his forces; one ranged widely, the other confined himself to fastnesses. Both different, but equal in death. Neither was allowed to escape dishonour nor to fall amidst the clash of weapons. With the loss of their feigned dignity, with the trappings of office stripped away, both were reduced to their true appearance and, with hands bound behind them, meekly they presented their necks to the drawn swords and begged for life and pardon. To such depths was their honour sunk! Those who of late directed such serried cohorts with a nod of the head, towards whom the balance of the hesitant world had already swung, fall not like foes before a victor, but like guilty men before a judge: he sentences with a word those whom he warred against as tyrants. Both their leaders perished: one voluntarily leapt from his ship into the waves, his own sword slew the other; one found a grave in the Alps, the other in the sea. Such solace the avenger offered to the murdered brothers: both contrivers of their slaughter are fallen; no different the sacrifice that appeases their imperial shades. These offerings he made to their tombs, and with a just out-pouring of blood placated the royal spirits of these two young men.

Those triumphs strengthened the rule of law and taught that gods move among men. From this let future ages learn

indomitum nihil esse pio tutumve nocenti.   100
nuntius ipse sui longas incognitus egit
praevento rumore vias, inopinus utrumque
perculit et clausos montes, ut plana, reliquit.
extruite immanes scopulos, attollite turres,
cingite vos fluviis, vastas opponite silvas,   105
Garganum Alpinis Appenninumque nivalem
permixtis sociate iugis et rupibus Haemum
addite Caucaseis, involvite Pelion Ossae,
non dabitis murum sceleri: qui vindicet, ibit.
omnia subsident meliori pervia causae.   110
   Nec tamen oblitus civem cedentibus atrox
partibus infremuit; non insultare iacenti
malebat: mitis precibus, pietatis abundans,
poenae parcus erat; paci non intulit iram;
post acies odiis idem qui terminus armis.   115
profuit hoc vincente capi, multosque subactos
aspera laturae commendavere catenae.
magnarum largitor opum, largitor honorum,
pronus et in melius gaudens convertere fata.
hinc amor, hinc validum devoto milite robur,   120
hinc natis mansura fides. hoc nobilis ortu
nasceris aequaeva cum maiestate creatus
nullaque privatae passus contagia sortis.
omnibus acceptis ultro te regia solum
protulit et patrio felix adolescis in ostro,   125
membraque vestitu numquam violata profano
in sacros cecidere sinus. Hispania patrem
auriferis eduxit aquis, te gaudet alumno
Bosphorus. Hesperio de limine surgit origo,
sed nutrix Aurora tibi. pro pignore tanto   130
certatur, geminus civem te vindicat axis.
Herculis et Bromii sustentat gloria Thebas,
haesit Apollineo Delos Latonia partu
Cretaque se iactat tenero reptata Tonanti:

107 permixtis PBΠ[1], permitto Em, pernices AΠ[2], Pyrenes *Barth.*, *Heins.*
126 violata PΠ, temerata ABΛ.

that nothing can withstand a good man, nothing protect the wicked. With no herald but himself, faster than word could travel, he covered long distances, unknown to his enemies, unlooked for he fell on both, and negotiated pathless mountains like plains. Pile up huge rocks, raise up towers, surround yourselves with rivers, set up vast forests as barriers, join Garganus and the snowy Appennine to the range of Alpine peaks, put Haemus on the Caucasian crags, top Ossa with Pelion, yet you will provide no refuge for the criminal: there will come one to punish. All these will subside and make way for the better cause.

And yet he did not, unmindful of his fellow-citizen, rage fiercely against the losing side; he chose not to trample on the fallen. Merciful he was to prayers, overflowing with love, sparing of punishment; he did not carry his anger over into time of peace. When the fighting was done, his hatred and his arms saw the same end. With him as conqueror, to be captured was a boon, and the chains that spoke of hardships to come aroused his pity for their wearers. Generous with his great riches, generous with honours, he was willing and happy to redress misfortunes. Hence sprang the love, hence the stout hearts of his devoted soldiers, hence the loyalty that would remain for his children.

With these antecedents you are nobly born; majesty was yours from birth; unsullied are you by the lot of a private citizen. All that you have came unsought; you alone are the child of the palace and happy your growth in inherited purple. Your body was never demeaned by profane clothing and the breast that received you was sacred. Spain with its gold-laden rivers brought forth your father: Bosphorus rejoices to have reared you. Your forebears arose from the Western edge of the world, but the land of the Dawn was your nurse. The honour of so great a trust is contested: the world's two parts claim you as its citizen. The glory of Hercules and Bacchus sustains Thebes; Latonian Delos stood firm at Apollo's birth; Crete boasts that there the infant Thunderer crawled: but

sed melior Delo, Dictaeis clarior oris 135
quae dedit hoc numen regio. non litora nostro
sufficerent angusta deo; nec inhospita Cynthi
saxa tuos artus duro laesere cubili:
adclinis genetrix auro, circumflua gemmis
in Tyrios enixa toros; ululata verendis 140
aula puerperiis. quae tunc documenta futuri?
quae voces avium? quanti per inane volatus?
quis vatum discursus erat? tibi corniger Hammon
et dudum taciti rupere silentia Delphi,
te Persae cecinere magi, te sensit Etruscus 145
augur et inspectis Babylonius horruit astris,
Chaldaei stupuere senes Cumanaque rursus
intonuit rupes, rabidae delubra Sibyllae.
nec te progenitum Cybeleius aere sonoro
lustravit Corybas: exercitus undique fulgens 150
adstitit; ambitur signis augustior infans,
sentit adorantes galeas, redditque ferocem
vagitum lituis. vitam tibi contulit idem
imperiumque dies: inter cunabula consul
proveheris, signas posito modo nomine fastos 155
donaturque tibi, qui te produxerat, annus.
ipsa Quirinali parvum te cinxit amictu
mater et ad primas docuit reptare curules.
uberibus sanctis inmortalique dearum
crescis adoratus gremio: tibi saepe Diana 160
Maenalios arcus venatricesque pharetras
suspendit, puerile decus; tu saepe Minervae
lusisti clipeo fulvamque impune pererrans
aegida tractasti blandos interritus angues;
saepe tuas etiam iam tum gaudente marito 165
velavit regina comas festinaque voti
praesumptum diadema dedit, tum lenibus ulnis
sustulit et magno porrexit ad oscula patri.
nec dilatus honos: mutatur principe Caesar;

---

137 angusta P², *vel* an(gusta) *add* Π¹, augusta *cett.*   153 lituis: lituus ε.
160 adoratus: odoratus E.   169 mutatur EΠA, mutatus B.

greater than Delos, more celebrated than the coast of Crete, is the region that gave us this divinity. No narrow shores would do for our god; the barren rocks of Cynthus did not bruise your limbs with their hard bed: your mother bedecked with jewels was brought to bed on a couch of gold, and gave you birth on Tyrian purple; a palace rang with her cries in her holy labour. What prophetic signs were given then? What songs of birds? How many their flights through the void? What activity among the prophets? For you horned Ammon and Delphi, long mute, broke their silence. The Persian magi sang of you, the Etruscan augur marked your advent, and the Babylonian trembled as he scanned the stars, the wise Chaldaeans stood amazed and the rock of Cumae, shrine of the frenzied Sibyl, thundered again. No Corybant of Cybele moved round you, newly-born, with clashing brass: a shining army stood all about you; this infant more august is surrounded by standards, beholds the worshipping helmets, and answers the trumpets with a bold cry. One day gave you both life and authority: in your cradle you are advanced to consul, you are entered in the calendar under the name but lately bestowed on you, and the year that gave you birth is consecrated to you. Your mother herself clothed your tiny form in the consul's robe, and taught you how to crawl to your first curule chair. Weaned at holy breasts, you grew, adored, on the lap of immortal goddesses: often did Diana do honour to your boyhood by fastening on you her Maenalian bow and her hunting-quiver; often you played with Minerva's shield and, unafraid, stroked the friendly snakes as you crawled unharmed on her tawny aegis. Even then to her husband's joy your mother often crowned your hair and, in eager anticipation of her wish, gave you the diadem in advance, then lifted you on gentle arms and held you up for your great father to kiss. Nor was the honour long deferred: Caesar be-

protinus aequaris fratri. non certius umquam   170
hortati superi, nullis praesentior aether
adfuit ominibus. tenebris involverat atra
lumen hiems densosque Notus collegerat imbres.
sed mox, cum solita miles te voce levasset,
nubila dissolvit Phoebus pariterque dabantur   175
sceptra tibi mundoque dies. caligine liber
Bosphorus adversam patitur Chalcedona cerni.
nec tantum vicina nitent, sed tota repulsis
nubibus exuitur Thrace, Pangaea renident
insuetosque palus radios Maeotia vibrat.   180
nec Boreas nimbos aut sol ardentior egit:
imperii lux illa fuit. praesagus obibat
cuncta nitor risitque tuo natura sereno.
visa etiam medio populis mirantibus audax
stella die, dubitanda nihil nec crine retuso   185
languida, sed quantus numeratur nocte Bootes,
emicuitque plagis alieni temporis hospes
ignis et agnosci potuit, cum luna lateret;
sive parens Augusta fuit, seu forte reluxit
divi sidus avi, seu te properantibus astris   190
cernere sol patiens caelum commune remisit.
adparet quid signa ferant. ventura potestas
claruit Ascanio, subita cum luce comarum
innocuus flagraret apex Phrygioque volutus
vertice fatalis redimiret tempora candor: 195
at tua caelestes inlustrant omina flammae.
talis ab Idaeis primaevus Iuppiter antris
possessi stetit arce poli famulosque recepit
natura tradente deos; lanugine nondum
vernabant vultus nec adhuc per colla fluebant   200
moturae convexa comae; tum scindere nubes
discebat fulmenque rudi torquere lacerto.
    Laetior augurio genitor natisque superbus
iam paribus duplici fultus consorte redibat

172 atra Emε, astra P, atris B.   189 forte: sponte B.   190 divi sidus avi seu
te Emε, divus avus seu te claris pr. B, divus avus fausta A, divus avus seu te
versu manco ΠP.

comes emperor; from this time on you are the equal of your brother. Never did the gods give their approval more clearly, never did heaven more surely manifest its presence by omens. A dark storm had veiled the light with darkness, and the South wind had accumulated thick masses of rain-cloud. But in a little while, when the soldiers had raised you up with time-honoured shout, Phoebus dispersed the clouds and in the same moment the sceptre was given to you and light to the world: as the darkness lifts, Bosphorus allows a glimpse of Chalcedon opposite. The brightness is not confined to the parts that border Constantinople, but all of Thrace is cleared with the scattering of the clouds, Pangaeus is refulgent and the pool of Maeotis shimmers with unfamiliar sunlight. It was not Boreas, not the radiant sun that dispelled the clouds: it was the light of empire; a prophetic glow bathed the world and all nature returned your brightness with its smile. To the wonderment of the peoples a bold star was seen at noon-day, a star quite unmistakable, not one that showed faintly with shortened ray, but as large as the Bearward seen at night in all its parts, and that star, strange and unseasonable, shed forth its light from the regions of the sky, and could be discerned, though the moon was hidden: it was either your imperial mother, or your deified grandfather's star that shone, or perhaps it was that the indulgent sun gave the freedom of heaven to all the stars that hastened to behold you. It is clear what these signs portend. Greatness to come was made plain for Ascanius, when of a sudden a tongue of flame lit up his hair and burned harmlessly; and the light of destiny, enveloping the Phrygian's head, wreathed his temples: but it is the fires of heaven that light your omens. So the infant Jupiter, issuing from the caves of Ida, took his stand upon the citadel of heaven, now his, and received the gods into his service from the hands of nature; the first down was not as yet upon his face, nor yet had the locks that would one day shake the heavens descended to his neck; then he was still learning how to rend the clouds and hurl his thunderbolt with prentice arm.

Heartened by the augury your father, proud of his sons

splendebatque pio complexus pignora curru.   205
haud aliter summo gemini cum patre Lacones,
progenies Ledaea, sedent: in utroque relucet
frater, utroque soror; simili chlamys effluit auro;
stellati pariter crines. iuvat ipse Tonantem
error et ambiguae placet ignorantia matri;   210
Eurotas proprios discernere nescit alumnos.
    Vt domus excepit reduces, ibi talia tecum
pro rerum stabili fertur dicione locutus:
    'Si tibi Parthorum solium Fortuna dedisset,
care puer, terrisque procul venerandus Eois   215
barbarus Arsacio consurgeret ore tiaras,
sufficeret sublime genus luxuque fluentem
deside nobilitas posset te sola tueri.
altera Romanae longe rectoribus aulae
condicio: virtute decet, non sanguine niti.   220
maior et utilior fato coniuncta potenti,
vile latens virtus. quid enim? submersa tenebris
proderit obscuro veluti sine remige puppis
vel lyra quae reticet vel qui non tenditur arcus.
hanc tamen haud quisquam, qui non agnoverit ante   225
semet et incertos animi placaverit aestus,
inveniet; longis illuc ambagibus itur.
disce orbi, quod quisque sibi. cum conderet artus
nostros, aetheriis miscens terrena, Prometheus,
sinceram patrio mentem furatus Olympo   230
continuit claustris indignantemque revinxit
et, cum non aliter possent mortalia fingi,
adiunxit geminas. illae cum corpore lapsae
intereunt, haec sola manet bustoque superstes
evolat. hanc alta capitis fundavit in arce   235
mandatricem operum prospecturamque labori;
illas inferius collo praeceptaque summae
passuras dominae digna statione locavit.
quippe opifex veritus confundere sacra profanis

208 simili ΕΠ, similis *cett.*   212 tecum: secum P.   214 dedisset: tulisset
Isengr. mg.   230 patrio: *dett. perpauci*, patri ΡΠΒΑ.

now equal in rank, returned leaning on his two partners, radiant as he embraced his children in the holy chariot. Just so do the Spartan twins, the sons of Leda, sit with their almighty father: each reflects the likeness of the other, each that of their sister; both are robed in identical gold; the hair of both is decked with stars. The very confusion pleases the Thunderer, and the puzzlement of the mother in her uncertainty is delightful to her; Eurotas does not know how to tell his own nurselings apart.

When they returned to the palace, there Theodosius is said to have spoken with you in this way, for the stable governing of the world: "If fortune, dear son, had given you the Parthian throne, and the barbarous tiara of the Arsacids that compels reverence in the distant lands of the East rose high upon your head, exalted birth would be enough and, even if you wallowed in luxury and sloth, noble lineage could defend you by itself. It is a very different matter for those who preside over the court of Rome. They should rely on virtue, not blood. Greater and more serviceable is the virtue that is coupled with destined power, virtue undisplayed is worthless. And why? If it is hidden in darkness it will do little good to its unknown owner, like a ship without a rower, a lyre that is silent, or a bow that is unbent. Yet this virtue none shall find who has not first come to know himself and controlled the uncertain waverings of his mind; the road to virtue is long and winding. Learn for the world what each man learns for himself. When Prometheus was framing our limbs, mixing earthly elements with divine, he stole pure reason from its Olympian home, bound it and imprisoned it against its will; and when it proved impossible to fashion mortal nature in any other way, he added two other parts. These fail and perish with the body: only the former endures and, undestroyed by the pyre, flies away. This he placed in the lofty citadel of the head to give direction to the work and cast its eye over the labour; the latter two he placed beneath the neck, where they belonged, to receive the orders of their mistress supreme. For the craftsman, afraid of mixing the sacred with the profane,

distribuit partes animae sedesque removit.   240
iram sanguinei regio sub pectore cordis
protegit imbutam flammis avidamque nocendi
praecipitemque sui. rabie succensa tumescit,
contrahitur tepefacta metu. cumque omnia secum
duceret et requiem membris vesana negaret,   245
invenit pulmonis opem madidumque furenti
praebuit, ut tumidae ruerent in mollia fibrae.
at sibi cuncta petens, nil conlatura cupido
in iecur et tractus imos compulsa recessit,
quae, velut immanis reserat dum belua rictus,   250
expleri pascique nequit: nunc verbere curas
torquet avaritiae, stimulis nunc flagrat amorum,
nunc gaudet, nunc maesta dolet satiataque rursus
exoritur caesaque redit pollentius hydra.
   'Hos igitur potuit si quis sedare tumultus,   255
inconcussa dabit purae sacraria menti.
tu licet extremos late dominere per Indos,
te Medus, te mollis Arabs, te Seres adorent,
si metuis, si prava cupis, si duceris ira,
servitii patiere iugum; tolerabis iniquas   260
interius leges. tunc omnia iure tenebis,
cum poteris rex esse tui. proclivior usus
in peiora datur suadetque licentia luxum
inlecebrisque effrena favet. tum vivere caste
asperius, cum prompta Venus; tum durius irae   265
consulitur, cum poena patet. sed comprime motus
nec tibi quid liceat, sed quid fecisse decebit
occurrat mentemque domet respectus honesti.
   'Hoc te praeterea crebro sermone monebo,
ut te totius medio telluris in ore   270
vivere cognoscas, cunctis tua gentibus esse
facta palam nec posse dari regalibus usquam
secretum vitiis; nam lux altissima fati
occultum nihil esse sinit, latebrasque per omnes

250 immanis EA, inmanis Π, immanes *cett.*   251 nequit B, velit *cett.*
253 dolet: silet *Isengr. mg.*   270 ore: orbe AΠ2P1.

separated the parts of the soul and set their seats apart. Beneath the breast the region of the heart, the source of the blood, shelters anger imbued with fire, anger yearning to do harm and of headlong impetuosity. Kindled by rage it swells, cooled by fear it shrinks. And, since it was drawing everything along with it and, in its madness, granting no rest to the body, he contrived the assistance of the lungs and provided their moisture to cool its fury, so that the swelling flesh might be mollified. But lust, wanting everything for itself, giving away nothing, was obliged to retire into the liver and the lowest parts, lust that while it bares its teeth like some savage beast, cannot be fed and satisfied: now with its lash it whips up the cares of avarice, now burns with the stings of love, now rejoices, now is downcast and sad, and, though replete, springs up afresh and returns with more strength than the chopped-up hydra.

"Whoever, then, can master these passions, will provide an inviolate temple for a right mind. Though your rule extend over farthest India, though the Mede, the effeminate Arab and the Chinese bow down to you, if you are afraid, if your appetites are depraved, if you are led by anger, then you will suffer the yoke of slavery, you will be subject to harsh laws within. Only when you can be sovereign over yourself will you be entitled to rule the world. The practice of vice tends to worse vices, unbridled freedom encourages excess and promotes indulgence. It is harder to live chastely, when love is at hand; more difficult to control anger when vengeance is easy. But quell these passions, let your thoughts be, not of what you can do, but of what it will befit you to have done, and let regard for what is honourable rule your mind.

"Of this too will I constantly remind you, that you may be aware that you live in full view of the whole earth: the things you do are observed by every nation and there can be no secret place anywhere for the vices of kings; for the light of the highest destiny allows nothing to be hidden: fame penetrates every cranny and explores each hidden retreat.

intrat et abstrusos explorat fama recessus. 275
  'Sis pius in primis; nam cum vincamur in omni
munere, sola deos aequat clementia nobis.
neu dubie suspectus agas neu falsus amicis
rumorumve avidus: qui talia curat, inanes
horrebit strepitus nulla non anxius hora. 280
non sic excubiae, non circumstantia pila
quam tutatur amor. non extorquebis amari:
hoc alterna fides, hoc simplex gratia donat.
nonne vides, operum quod se pulcherrimus ipse
mundus amore liget, nec vi conexa per aevum 285
conspirent elementa sibi? quod limite Phoebus
contentus medio, contentus litore pontus
et, qui perpetuo terras ambitque vehitque,
nec premat incumbens oneri nec cesserit aer?
qui terret, plus ipse timet: sors ista tyrannis 290
convenit. invideant claris fortesque trucident,
muniti gladiis vivant saeptique venenis,
ancipites habeant arces trepidique minentur:
tu civem patremque geras, tu consule cunctis,
non tibi, nec tua te moveant, sed publica vota. 295
  'In commune iubes si quid censesve tenendum,
primus iussa subi: tunc observantior aequi
fit populus nec ferre negat, cum viderit ipsum
auctorem parere sibi. componitur orbis
regis ad exemplum, nec sic inflectere sensus 300
humanos edicta valent quam vita regentis.
mobile mutatur semper cum principe vulgus.
  'His tamen effectis neu fastidire minores
neu pete praescriptos homini transcendere fines.
inquinat egregios adiuncta superbia mores. 305
non tibi tradidimus dociles servire Sabaeos,
Armeniae dominum non te praefecimus orae,
nec damus Assyriam, tenuit quam femina, gentem.
Romani, qui cuncta diu rexere, regendi,

---

275 abstrusos Em *Isengr. mg.*, obstrusos PA, obtrusos BΠ.   278 amicis:
amicus P1.   285 conexa EP, convexa B, connexa *cett.*   298 negat EmϵΠ,
vetat PAB.

"Be loving above all else; for though we fall behind in every other gift, it is mercy alone that makes us equal with the gods. Be not doubtful or suspicious of friends, be true to them and pay no heed to rumours: he who gives heed to these will start at every sound and know anxiety at every hour. No body-guard, no ring of javelins give such defence as love. Love will not be compelled: it is the gift of mutual loyalty, the gift of dis-interested esteem. Do you not see how the universe, the fairest of all things made, holds itself together with love, nor how the elements are in eternal harmony, unconstrained by force? How Phoebus is content with his middle course, the sea with its shore, and how the air, which is forever both around and under the earth, neither crushes it as it lies upon it nor has ever failed to support its weight? The man who frightens others is more afraid himself: that fate suits tyrants. Let them resent the famous, kill the brave, live defended by swords and ringed about by poisons, keep to untrustworthy citadels, and threaten as they tremble. Conduct yourself like a citizen and a father, take thought for all, not for yourself, and let the people's wishes move you, not your own.

"If you make some general edict or decree some ob-servance, be the first to submit to your own commands: then does the people show more regard for justice and accept its responsibilities, when it sees the law-giver obedient to him-self. The world conforms to the example of a king, and no edicts have such a power to influence the feelings of men as the life of their ruler. The fickle mob forever changes with its prince.

"But having done all this, be not disdainful of those beneath you, nor seek to transgress the limits set for mankind. An excellent character is defiled by the addition of pride. I have not delivered docile Sabaeans to your rule, not made you master of the Armenian land; it is not the Assyrian people, once ruled by a woman, I give you now. You are to rule the Romans, who long have ruled the world, who tolerated neither the pride

qui nec Tarquinii fastus nec iura tulere   310
Caesaris. annales veterum delicta loquuntur:
haerebunt maculae. quis non per saecula damnat
Caesareae portenta domus? quem dira Neronis
funera, quem rupes Caprearum taetra latebit
incesto possessa seni? victura feretur   315
gloria Traiani, non tam quod Tigride victo
nostra triumphati fuerint provincia Parthi,
alta quod invectus fractis Capitolia Dacis,
quam patriae quod mitis erat. ne desine tales,
nate, sequi. si bella canant, prius agmina duris   320
exerce studiis et saevo praestrue Marti.
non brumae requies, non hibernacula segnes
enervent torpore manus. ponenda salubri
castra loco; praebenda vigil custodia vallo.
disce, ubi denseri cuneos, ubi cornua tendi   325
aequius aut iterum flecti; quae montibus aptae,
quae campis acies; quae fraudi commoda vallis,
quae via difficilis. fidit si moenibus hostis,
tum tibi murali libretur machina pulsu;
saxa rota; praeceps aries protectaque portas   330
testudo feriat; ruat emersura iuventus
effossi per operta soli. si longa moretur
obsidio, tum vota cave secura remittas
inclusumve putes; multis damnosa fuere
gaudia; dispersi pereunt somnove soluti;   335
saepius incautae nocuit victoria turbae.
neu tibi regificis tentoria larga redundent
deliciis, neve imbelles ad signa ministros
Luxuries armata trahat. neu flantibus Austris
neu pluviis cedas, neu defensura calorem   340
aurea summoveant rapidos umbracula soles.
inventis utere cibis. solabere partes
aequali sudore tuas: si collis iniquus,
primus ini; silvam si caedere provocat usus,

---

315 *invenitur hic versus in paucis tantum deterioribus: restituit Bentinus in editione Isengrinii.* 320 canant: tonant B, vocant *Heins.* 325 denseri E, densus erit AΠBP1. 330 rota: rotet Λ, rotat Π, rotans *Heins.* protectaque: proiectaque Π2 *Isengr. mg.* 339 flantibus austris: flatibus austri E.

of Tarquin nor the laws of Caesar. The annals tell of the crimes of the ancients: the pollution will remain. Who, while ages last, does not condemn the horrors of the Julian house? Who will not know of the savage murders of Nero, who of the foul rock of Capri, home of that depraved old man? But the eternal glory of Trajan will be related, not so much because he conquered the Tigris and triumphed over Parthia, now our province, nor because he rode in procession up the steep Capitol for crushing the Dacians, as because he showed loving-kindness to his country. Cease not to follow such examples, my son.

"If the trumpets of war sound, first train your forces with rigorous exercises and make ready for cruel war. Do not allow the winter-break and life in barracks to sap the strength of the troops, or make them sluggish with inactivity. The camp must be pitched on a healthy site; an alert picket must be provided for the rampart. Learn in what situations it is better to contract your companies, to extend the wings or draw them in again; what formations suit mountainous, what level, terrains; what valley may lend itself to ambush, what road is difficult. If your enemy places his trust in walls, then aim your artillery to pound his ramparts; hurl rocks; let the thrusting head of the battering-ram and the shielded testudo assail his gates; let your men burst forth from a mine they have dug through the bowels of the earth. Should the siege prove long, then take care not to relax your intention in false security, or think the besieged held fast; such rejoicing has proved the ruin of many; men are lost when scattered or asleep; victory has often brought destruction to a host when off its guard. Have no huge marquees over-flowing with comforts fit for a king, nor permit armed Luxury to follow the standards with an unwarlike retinue. Do not give in to the South wind's blasts nor to the rain, nor, as your protection against the heat, have golden parasols to ward off the burning sun. You will take what food you find. You will encourage your men if your sweat equals theirs: if the hill is steep, be the first to climb; if the situation calls for the levelling

sumpta ne pudeat quercum stravisse bipenni.   345
calcatur si pigra palus, tuus ante profundum
pertemptet sonipes. fluvios tu protere curru
haerentes glacie, liquidos tu scinde natatu.
nunc eques in medias equitum te consere turmas:
nunc pedes adsistas pediti. tum promptius ibunt   350
te socio, tum conspicuus gratusque geretur
sub te teste labor.' dicturum plura parentem
voce subis: 'equidem, faveant modo numina coeptis,
haec effecta dabo, nec me fratrique tibique
dissimilem populi commissaque regna videbunt.   355
sed cur non potius, verbis quae disseris, usu
experior? gelidas certe nunc tendis in Alpes.
duc tecum comitem; figant, sine, nostra tyrannum
spicula; pallescat nostro, sine, barbarus arcu.
Italiamne feram furiis praedonis acerbi   360
subiectam? patiar Romam servire clienti?
usque adeone puer? nec me polluta potestas
nec pia cognati tanget vindicta cruoris?
per strages equitare libet. da protinus arma.
cur annos obicis? pugnae cur arguor impar?   365
aequalis mihi Pyrrhus erat, cum Pergama solus
verteret et patri non degeneraret Achilli.
denique si princeps castris haerere nequibo,
vel miles veniam.' delibat dulcia nati
oscula miratusque refert: 'laudanda petisti;   370
sed festinus amor. veniet robustior aetas:
ne propera. necdum decimas emensus aristas
adgrederis metuenda viris: vestigia magnae
indolis agnosco. fertur Pellaeus, Eoum
qui domuit Porum, cum prospera saepe Philippi   375
audiret, laetos inter flevisse sodales
nil sibi vincendum patris virtute relinqui.
hos video motus. fas sit promittere patri:
tantus eris; nostro nec debes regna favori,

348 haerentes: horrentes PΠ².   350 pediti: equiti B.   353 subis: subit P.
367 verteret: sterneret P¹.   368 princeps castris: castris princeps Π.
371 amor: honor B.   378 sit: est A.

of a forest, do not be above taking up the axe and felling the oak-tree. If the route lies over a heavy swamp, let your steed first test its depth. Drive your chariot over frozen rivers, swim across running water. Now mounted, ride into the midst of the cavalry squadrons; now on foot support the infantry. With you as their comrade they will press on the more readily, gallant and glad will be the action performed under your eyes."

You break into your father's unfinished discourse with these words: "Certainly, if the gods assist my efforts, all this I will do, and the peoples and kingdoms entrusted to me will see that I am no different from my brother and yourself. But why do I not rather try out in practice the things you teach me? You are marching now upon the wintry Alps. Take me along with you; let my arrows pierce the tyrant; let the barbarian grow pale at my bow. Am I to allow Italy to be a victim to the madness of a cruel adventurer? to allow Rome to be the slave of a dependent? Do you think me still such a child? Shall I remain unmoved by the profanation of imperial power or the vengeance due to a kinsman's murder? I long to career through the carnage. Give me arms now. Why is my age an objection? Why am I said to be unequal to the fight? Pyrrhus was just my age when he overthrew Troy single-handed and proved a true son of his father Achilles. In short, if there is no room for me in your camp as prince, I will come even as a soldier."

Theodosius tasted his son's sweet kisses and full of admiration replied: "Your wishes do you credit; but your love of battle is premature. Your years will soon mature: contain yourself. You have not yet completed your tenth summer and already you are for tackling dangers that would daunt grown men: I see the signs of a noble nature. The man from Pella who vanquished Porus in the east is said, as often as he heard of Philip's successes, to have wept to his rejoicing friends that his father's valour left him nothing to conquer. I see the same desires. May a father be allowed to prophesy: you will be just as great. It is to no favour of mine that you owe your kingdom —

quae tibi iam natura dedit. sic mollibus olim   380
stridula ducturum pratis examina regem
nascentem venerantur apes et publica mellis
iura petunt traduntque favos; sic pascua parvus
vindicat et necdum firmatis cornibus audax
iam regit armentum vitulus. sed proelia differ   385
in iuvenem patiensque meum cum fratre tuere
me bellante locum. vos impacatus Araxes,
vos celer Euphrates timeat, sit Nilus ubique
vester et emisso quidquid sol imbuit ortu.
si pateant Alpes, habeat si causa secundos   390
iustior eventus, aderis partesque receptas
suscipies, animosa tuas ut Gallia leges
audiat et nostros aequus modereris Hiberos.
tunc ego securus fati laetusque laborum
discedam, vobis utrumque regentibus axem.   395
  'Interea Musis animus, dum mollior, instet
et quae mox imitere legat; nec desinat umquam
tecum Graia loqui, tecum Romana vetustas.
antiquos evolve duces, adsuesce futurae
militiae, Latium retro te confer in aevum.   400
libertas quaesita placet? mirabere Brutum.
perfidiam damnas? Metti satiabere poenis.
triste rigor nimius? Torquati despue mores.
mors impensa bonum? Decios venerare ruentes.
vel solus quid fortis agat, te ponte soluto   405
oppositus Cocles, Muci te flamma docebit.
quid mora perfringat, Fabius, quid rebus in artis
dux gerat, ostendet Gallorum strage Camillus.
discitur hinc nullos meritis obsistere casus:
prorogat aeternam feritas tibi Punica famam,   410
Regule; successus superant adversa Catonis.
discitur hinc quantum paupertas sobria possit:
pauper erat Curius, reges cum vinceret armis;
pauper Fabricius, Pyrrhi cum sperneret aurum;

387 me: te P.   405 vel: vir *Isengr. mg.*   412 hinc II, in *cett.*

nature has already given you it. Just so do bees do reverence to their new-born king, future leader of their humming swarms through lush meadows, and invite him to exercise public jurisdiction over the honey and give up to him their combs; just so a young steer claims his stake in the pasture and boldly dominates the herd, though his horns are still tender. But put off your battles till you are older, be patient and, with your brother, keep my place while I wage war. Be it your task, my sons, to strike terror into untamed Araxes and swift Euphrates, may the whole Nile be yours, and all that is warmed by the rising sun. If I find a way through the Alps, if the juster cause is attended by favourable outcome, you shall come to me and receive the lands that I win back, that proud Gaul may give ear to your laws and that you may rule with equity over our own Spanish people. Then I, indifferent to fate and rejoicing in my labours, shall take my leave, while you, my sons, rule West and East.

"Till then, while your mind is tender, cultivate the Muses, and let your reading supply examples for you soon to follow; never cease to hear the story of Greece nor the story of ancient Rome. Unfold the tales of warriors of old; train yourself for coming service; travel back in time to the age of the Latins. Does the quest for liberty give you pleasure? you will marvel at Brutus. Do you condemn treachery? you will be satisfied with the punishment of Mettus. Is undue severity cause for grief? spurn the stern nature of Torquatus. Is the supreme sacrifice a blessing? honour the Decii rushing to their death. What a brave man may do even single-handed, the stand of Horatius Cocles at the broken bridge and the flame of Mucius Scaevola will teach you. What obstacles a delaying tactic can break down Fabius will reveal to you, and Camillus, by the slaughter of the Gauls, what a general can do in a tight corner. One may learn from these that nothing that can happen stands in the way of merit: the cruelty of Carthage makes your name live throughout all ages, Regulus; the failure of Cato is greater than any success. One may learn from these the power of poverty and sobriety. Curius was poor when he conquered kings in battle; Fabricius was poor when he rejected the gold of Pyrrhus;

sordida dictator flexit Serranus aratra.   415
lustratae lictore casae fascesque salignis
postibus affixi; collectae consule messes
et sulcata diu trabeato rura colono.'
haec genitor praecepta dabat: velut ille carinae
longaevus rector, variis quem saepe procellis   420
exploravit hiems, ponto iam fessus et annis
aequoreas alni nato commendat habenas
et casus artesque docet: quo dextra regatur
sidere; quo fluctus possit moderamine falli;
quae nota nimborum; quae fraus infida sereni;   425
quid sol occiduus prodat; quo saucia vento
decolor iratos attollat Cynthia vultus.
   Adspice nunc, quacumque micas, seu circulus Austri
magne parens, gelidi seu te meruere Triones,
adspice: completur votum. iam natus adaequat   430
te meritis et, quod magis est optabile, vincit,
subnixus Stilichone tuo, quem fratribus ipse
discedens clipeum defensoremque dedisti.
pro nobis nihil ille pati nullumque recusat
discrimen temptare sui, non dura viarum,   435
non incerta maris; Libyae squalentis harenas
audebit superare pedes madidaque cadente
Pleiade Gaetulas intrabit navita Syrtes.
   Hunc tamen in primis populos lenire feroces
et Rhenum pacare iubes. volat ille citatis   440
vectus equis nullaque latus stipante caterva,
aspera nubiferas qua Raetia porrigit Alpes,
pergit et hostiles (tanta est fiducia) ripas
incomitatus adit. totum properare per amnem
attonitos reges humili cervice videres.   445
ante ducem nostrum flavam sparsere Sygambri
caesariem pavidoque orantes murmure Franci
procubuere solo: iuratur Honorius absens
imploratque tuum supplex Alamannia nomen.

422 alni: olim P.   432 *versus deest in libris scriptis qui exstant: primus ex-*
hibuit Bentinus.   438 navita syrtes Π *Isengr. mg.*, sirtibus undas PBΛ,
syrtibus undas A.   440 Rhenum: regnum Π1.

Serranus as dictator guided the muddy plough. Poor cottages were attended by the lictor and the fasces were hung on doorposts of willow; harvests were gathered in by consuls and for a long time the fields were furrowed by farmers in consular robes."

These precepts the father imparted: in the same way an aged ship's master, whom winter with its shifting squalls has often tested, now worn-out by sea-faring and old age, hands over the watery reins of his ship to his son and teaches him the dangers and skills: by what star the hand may be guided; by what use of the rudder the waves may be cheated; what is the sign of storms; what treacherous promise the clear sky holds; what the setting sun reveals; what wind it is that disfigures the moon so that the face she holds up is pale and angry. See now, great father, wherever you are shining, whether the zone of the Southern sky or the chilly Plough has won your company, see: your wish is fulfilled. Your son now equals you in merit and, what is even more to be desired, excels you, stayed on the support of your beloved Stilicho, whom at your departing you gave to be shield and defender to the brothers. On our behalf there is no hardship he declines to endure, no danger to attempt, no road too rough, no sea too risky; he will dare to cross the sands of parched Libya on foot and take his ship through the Gaetulian Syrtes when the watery Pleiad is setting.

But first you bid him quell fierce peoples and subdue the Rhine. He races, carried on swift horses, with no company at his side and makes his way where harsh Raetia stretches out the cloud-girt Alps and — such is his confidence — approaches the hostile banks alone. Then all along the river you might have seen its chieftains thunderstruck bow down their necks. Before our leader the Sygambri strewed their yellow locks and the Franks, murmuring fearful prayers, prostrated themselves upon the ground: they swear by the absent Honorius and Germany on her knees calls upon your name. The wild Bastarnae came,

Bastarnae venere truces, venit accola silvae 450
Bructerus Hercyniae latisque paludibus exit
Cimber et ingentes Albim liquere Cherusci.
accipit ille preces varias tardeque rogatus
adnuit et magno pacem pro munere donat.
nobilitant veteres Germanica foedera Drusos, 455
Marte sed ancipiti, sed multis cladibus empta.
quis victum meminit sola formidine Rhenum?
quod longis alii bellis potuere mereri,
hoc tibi dat Stilichonis iter. post otia Galli
limitis, hortaris Graias fulcire ruinas. 460
Ionium tegitur velis ventique laborant
tot curvare sinus servaturasque Corinthum
prosequitur facili Neptunus gurgite classes,
et puer, Isthmiaci iam pridem litoris exul,
secura repetit portus cum matre Palaemon. 465
plaustra cruore natant: metitur pellita iuventus:
pars morbo, pars ense perit. non lustra Lycaei,
non Erymantheae iam copia sufficit umbrae
innumeris exusta rogis, nudataque ferro
sic flagrasse suas laetantur Maenala silvas. 470
excutiat cineres Ephyre, Spartanus et Arcas
tutior exangues pedibus proculcet acervos
fessaque pensatis respiret Graecia poenis!
gens, qua non Scythicos diffusior ulla Triones
incoluit, cui parvus Athos angustaque Thrace, 475
cum transiret, erat, per te viresque tuorum
fracta ducum lugetque sibi iam rara superstes,
et, quorum turbae spatium vix praebuit orbis,
uno colle latent. sitiens inclusaque vallo
ereptas quaesivit aquas, quas hostibus ante 480
contiguas alio Stilicho deflexerat actu
mirantemque novas ignota per avia valles
iusserat averso fluvium migrare meatu.
obvia quid mirum vinci, cum barbarus ultro

466 plaustra ε, castra *cett.*   481 actu: arcu **PB**.

the Bructeri who dwell in the forest of Hercynia, the Cimbri came out from the wide marshes, and the mighty Cherusci left the Elbe. He listens to their several prayers, consents to their belated request and bestows on them the great gift of peace. The Drusi of old were ennobled by German pacts, but they were purchased in the wavering tide of war with many a defeat. Who can recall when Rhine was conquered by fear alone? What others could only win by lengthy wars, this the journey of Stilicho bestows on you.

When peace was established on the frontier of Gaul, you urge him to prevent the collapse of Greece. The Ionian sea is covered with ships and the winds are hard put to it to swell so many sails: Neptune with willing stream attends the fleet that will save Corinth, and the boy Palaemon, long an exile from the Isthmian shore, and his carefree mother make again for the harbour. The wagons are awash with blood: the skin-clad warriors are mown down: some perish by disease, some by the sword. The forests of Lycaeus and the abundant shade of Erymanthus have been burnt up and no longer suffice to fuel the countless pyres: Maenalus, stripped bare by the axe, is glad that her woods have blazed in such a cause. Let Ephyre shake off the ashes, let Spartan and Arcadian in greater safety trample underfoot the heaps of pallid corpses, let weary Greece draw breath again, since due punishment has been exacted! The race, than which no other has ever inhabited a wider tract of the Scythian north, for which Athos was too small, Thrace too narrow, as it passed across, is finished, and, crushed by you and the strength of your generals, its meagre survivor mourns itself, and they whose host the world could scarcely contain can hide upon a single hill. Confined within their rampart, thirstily they sought the water of which they were deprived: for Stilicho had turned aside by a different channel the water previously accessible to his enemy, and ordered the stream to flow with altered course through strange and devious places, wondering at the unfamiliar valleys. What wonder is it that obstacles are sur-

iam cupiat servire tibi? tua Sarmata discors   485
sacramenta petit; proiecta pelle Gelonus
militat; in Latios ritus transistis, Alani.
   Ut fortes in Marte viros animisque paratos,
sic iustos in pace legis longumque tueris
electos, crebris nec succedentibus urges.   490
iudicibus notis regimur, fruimurque quietis
militiaeque bonis, ceu bellatore Quirino,
ceu placido moderante Numa. non imminet ensis:
nullae nobilium caedes, non crimina vulgo
texuntur; patria maestus non truditur exul;   495
impia continui cessant augmenta tributi;
non infelices tabulae; non hasta refixas
vendit opes; avida sector non voce citatur,
nec tua privatis crescunt aeraria damnis.
munificus largi, sed non et prodigus, auri.   500
perdurat non empta fides nec pectora merces
adligat. ipsà suo pro pignore castra laborant;
te miles nutritor amat. quae denique Romae
cura tibi! quam fixa manet reverentia patrum!
firmatur senium iuris priscamque resumunt   505
canitiem leges emendanturque vetustae
acceduntque novae. talem sensere Solonem
res Pandioniae; sic armipotens Lacedaemon
despexit muros rigido munita Lycurgo.
quae sub te vel causa brevis vel iudicis error   510
neglegitur? dubiis quis litibus addere finem
iustior et mersum latebris educere verum?
quae pietas quantusque rigor tranquillaque magni
vis animi nulloque levis terrore moveri
nec nova mirari facilis! quam docta facultas   515
ingenii linguaeque modus! responsa verentur
legati gravibusque latet sub moribus aetas.
   Quantus in ore pater radiat! quam torva voluptas
frontis et augusti maiestas grata pudoris!

486 pelle EmϵA *Isengr. mg.*, tibique P, fraude P¹mg.ΠΒ.   498 avida Eϵ,
avidas ΠΠ, avidis AB. sector Em, emptor *cett.*   500 largi Π¹, laudis *cett.*
509 *hunc versum exhibuit primus Isengrinius. deest in mss. praeter duos*
inferioris notae.

mounted, when the barbarians long to serve you of their own free will? The strife-torn Sarmatian asks to swear allegiance to you; the Gelonian casts off his pelt and serves with your army; you Alans have adopted Roman customs.

As in war you choose brave men of willing spirit, so in peace you choose just men, maintain them long in office once selected, and are not constantly replacing them with others. We know our judges, we enjoy the blessings both of war and peace: it is as though the warlike Romulus and the peaceful Numa were governing us together. The sword poses no threat: there is no massacre of the nobles, no charges trumped up against the lowly; no exile is driven sorrowing from his country; vicious increases in the everlasting taxes come to an end; no lists of luckless men proscribed; no sales of confiscated goods; no bidder is summoned by the greedy voice of the auctioneer, nor does your treasury swell at the expense of private citizens. You are generous with your ample fortune, yet not prodigal of it. Unbought allegiance endures; hope of gain does not bind the heart. The camp exerts itself in the service of its nursling; the love of the soldiers who reared you is yours.

And then, how great is your regard for Rome! How constant the reverence you bear the Senate! The decay of justice is repaired, laws recover their old authority; outdated statutes are emended, new ones are added. The Athenian state found in Solon just such a one as you; just so did warlike Sparta despise defensive walls, fortified by the unbending Lycurgus. Under your rule, what trifling case, what judge's error is overlooked? Who shows more justice in determining difficult cases and in rescuing truth sunk in obscurity? What devotion, what constancy and tranquil strength of mind, not lightly moved by any fear, nor quick to marvel at things new! What ease and learning in your wit, how guarded your tongue! Ambassadors receive your answers with reverent awe and the gravity of your bearing belies your years.

How your great father shines forth from your face! How stern yet how charming your brow, how pleasing the majesty

iam patrias imples galeas; iam cornus avita 520
temptatur vibranda tibi; promittitur ingens
dextra rudimentis Romanaque vota moratur.
quis decor, incedis quotiens clipeatus et auro
squameus et rutilus cristis et casside maior!
sic, cum Threicia primum sudaret in hasta, 525
flumina laverunt puerum Rhodopeia Martem.
quae vires iaculis vel, cum Gortynia tendis
spicula, quam felix arcus certique petitor
vulneris et iussum mentiri nescius ictum!
scis, quo more Cydon, qua dirigat arte sagittas 530
Armenius, refugo quae sit fiducia Partho.
sic Amphioniae pulcher sudore palaestrae
Alcides pharetras Dircaeaque tela solebat
praetemptare feris olim domitura Gigantes
et pacem latura polo, semperque cruentus 535
ibat et Alcmenae praedam referebat ovanti.
caeruleus tali prostratus Apolline Python
implicuit fractis moritura volumina silvis.
   Cum vectaris equo simulacraque Martia ludis,
quis mollis sinuare fugas, quis tendere contum 540
acrior aut subitos melior flexisse recursus?
non te Massagetae, non gens exercita campo
Thessala, non ipsi poterunt aequare bimembres.
vix comites alae, vix te suspensa sequuntur
agmina ferventesque tument post terga dracones. 545
utque tuis primum sonipes calcaribus arsit,
ignescunt patulae nares, non sentit harenas
ungula discussaeque iubae sparguntur in armos;
turbantur phalerae, spumosis morsibus aurum
fumat, anhelantes exundant sanguine gemmae. 550
ipse labor pulvisque decet confusaque motu
caesaries; vestis radiato murice solem
combibit, ingesto crispatur purpura vento.
si dominus legeretur equis, tua posceret ultro

529 iussum BΛ, visum PAΠ². 543 bimembres: biformes B. 550 exundant: exudant P.

of your imperial modesty! Your father's helmet fits you already; now your grandfather's spear is being tested by you for throwing; these exercises give promise of a strong right-hand and Rome is impatient for the fulfilment of its wishes. How handsome when you march with shield and gold-scaled armour, glowing beneath your plumes, made taller by the helmet! So the young Mars as he bathed in the rivers of Rhodope, when first he practised with the Thracian spear. What strength behind your javelin thrusts, or, when you shoot Cretan arrows, how accurate your bow that never fails to make a wound and cannot miss the desired target! The Cretan method, the Armenian skill in archery, are known to you, and the confidence of the Parthian in retreat. So Hercules, comely with the sweat of the Theban wrestling-school upon him, used to practise upon wild beasts with arrows that would one day tame Giants and bring peace to heaven; in all his goings he was blood-stained, and ever brought back his prey to the applauding Alcmena. No different was Apollo when he laid low the livid Python that in its death-throes folded its coils around whole forests and broke them down.

When you take horse and your sport is the mimicry of war, who quicker to effect the smooth retreat, to deliver the javelin, or who better at wheeling back again in unexpected recovery? The Massagetae, the Thessalians for all their practice in the field, even the Centaurs themselves, none is a match for you. The squadrons and the swift columns that escort you can scarcely keep up, and the wind fills the glowing dragon-standards streaming behind. The moment your steed feels the smart of your spurs, he widens his nostrils and breathes fire, his hooves scarcely disturb the sand and his flying mane overspreads his neck; his trappings jangle, the golden bit reeks and foams beneath his champing, his jewelled harness heaves and drips with blood. The very toil and dust, the movement and disorder of your hair, all suit you well; your garments of radiant purple drink up the sunlight, its rich shade is ruffled by the action of the wind. If horses chose their owners, Arion reared in

verbera Nereidum stabulis nutritus Arion   555
serviretque tuis, contempto Castore, frenis
Cyllarus et flavum Xanthus sprevisset Achillem;
ipse tibi famulas praeberet Pegasus alas
portaretque libens melioraque pondera passus
Bellerophonteas indignaretur habenas.   560
quin etiam velox Aurorae nuntius Aethon,
qui fugat hinnitu stellas roseoque domatur
Lucifero, quotiens equitem te cernit ab astris,
invidet inque tuis mavult spumare lupatis.
    Nunc quoque quos habitus, quantae miracula pompae   565
vidimus, Ausonio cum iam succinctus amictu
per Ligurum populos solito conspectior ires
atque inter niveas alte veherere cohortes,
obnixisque simul pubes electa lacertis
sidereum gestaret onus. sic numina Memphis   570
in vulgus proferre solet: penetralibus exit
effigies, brevis illa quidem, sed plurimus infra
liniger imposito suspirat vecte sacerdos
testatus sudore deum; Nilotica sistris
ripa sonat Phariosque modos Aegyptia ducit   575
tibia; summissis admugit cornibus Apis.
omnis nobilitas, omnis tua sacra frequentat
Thybridis et Latii suboles; convenit in unum
quidquid in orbe fuit procerum, quibus auctor honoris
vel tu vel genitor. numeroso consule consul   580
cingeris et socios gaudes admittere patres.
illustri te prole Tagus, te Gallia doctis
civibus et toto stipavit Roma senatu.
portatur iuvenum cervicibus aurea sedes
ornatuque novo gravior deus. asperat Indus   585
velamenta lapis pretiosaque fila smaragdis
ducta virent; amethystus inest et fulgor Hiberus
temperat arcanis hyacinthi caerula flammis.
nec rudis in tali suffecit gratia textu;

---

565 nunc: tunc B.   573 inposito Π, imposita P, et posita ABΛ. vecte Π[1],
veste Π[2]PABΛ.

the stables of the Nereids would have begged for the touch of your whip, Cyllarus would have spurned Castor and obeyed your reins, Xanthus would have disdained golden-haired Achilles; Pegasus himself would have placed his wings at your service, would gladly have borne you, and, having carried a more precious load, would have chafed under the reins of a Bellerophon. Why, even Aethon, swift messenger of dawn, who chases away the stars with his neigh and is the mount of rosy Lucifer, whenever from the stars he sees you on your horse, feels jealous and would rather fleck your bit with foam.

Now, moreover, what robes, what a wonderful procession did we see as lately you passed among the people of Liguria, dressed in the trabea of Italy, more striking even than usual, and were borne aloft in the midst of your troops in snowy white, and chosen youths together offered their shoulders to support the heavenly burden. Thus Memphis is wont to bring out her gods for all to see: the image comes forth from its shrine, small to be sure but, under it, full many a linen-clad priest pants beneath the pole he carries and proves by his efforts that this is a god; the banks of Nile resound to their rattles, the Egyptian flute leads the Pharian chants; Apis puts down his horns and roars.

All the nobles, all the youth of Rome and Latium attend your ceremonies; the most exalted on earth, who owe their honours either to you or to your father, assemble together. Consul, you are flanked by many a consul, and you rejoice to receive the company of the Senators. The Tagus surrounded you with its famous sons, Gaul with its native scholars, Rome with its whole senate. The golden chair and its divine occupant, weightier because of his new regalia, are borne on the necks of youths. Indian stones bead the robe and the costly fine-spun stuff is green with emeralds; amethysts are worked in and the brightness of Spanish gold tempers the blue of the hyacinth with its hidden fires. Nor was the simple beauty of such a web considered enough; embroidery enhances its worth and the

auget acus meritum picturatumque metallis   590
vivit opus: multa glomerantur iaspide vultus
et variis spirat Nereia baca figuris.
quae tantum potuit digitis mollire rigorem
ambitiosa colus? vel cuius pectinis arte
traxerunt solidae gemmarum stamina telae?   595
invia quis calidi scrutatus stagna profundi
Tethyos invasit gremium? quis divitis algae
germina flagrantes inter quaesivit harenas?
quis iunxit lapides ostro? quis miscuit ignes
Sidonii Rubrique maris? tribuere colorem   600
Phoenices, Seres subtegmina, pondus Hydaspes.
hoc si Maeonias cinctu graderere per urbes,
in te pampineos transferret Lydia thyrsos,
in te Nysa choros, dubitassent orgia Bacchi
cui furerent, irent blandae sub vincula tigres.   605
talis Erythraeis intextus nebrida gemmis
Liber agit currus et Caspia flectit eburnis
colla iugis: Satyri circum crinemque solutae
Maenades adstringunt hederis victricibus Indos;
ebrius hostili velatur palmite Ganges.   610

    Auspice mox laetum sonuit clamore tribunal
te fastos ineunte quater. sollemnia ludit
omina Libertas; deductum Vindice morem
Lex celebrat, famulusque iugo laxatus erili
ducitur et grato remeat securior ictu.   615
tristis condicio pulsata fronte recedit;
in civem rubuere genae, tergoque removit
verbera permissi felix iniuria voti.

    Prospera Romuleis sperantur tempora rebus
in nomen ventura tuum. praemissa futuris   .   620
dant exempla fidem: quotiens te cursibus aevi
praefecit, totiens accessit laurea patri.
ausi Danubium quondam tranare Gruthungi
in lintres fregere nemus; ter mille ruebant

591 multa E, multaque *cett.* glomerantur: remorantur Em, orantur Π1,
ornantur Π2A, ortantur B, honeratur P, animatur *Heins.*, animantur *Mark-
land* (*Stat. 1.1.19*), glomerantur *temptavi*: *vide Athenaeum 32 (1954) 393
sqq.*   602 cinctu B, cum tu P, vultu EmΠA, cultu *dett.*   604 dubitassent:
dubitarent BΠ.   611 auspice E, aspice *cett.*   614 laxatus: lassatus AΠ2,
laxatur B.

work is vivid with pictures traced in metal threads: portraits throng together in a wealth of jasper and the sea-pearl comes to life in many a pattern. What ambitious distaff was able with the fingers' art to give softness to materials so hard? What comb, what sturdy looms combined their skill to fashion the jewelled threads into cloth? Who explored the pathless pools of the warm sea and plundered the bosom of Tethys? Who sought out the seed-pearls of rich sea-weed amidst the burning sands? Who joined the precious stones to the purple? Who mingled the glowing colours of the Red Sea and the Sidonian? Phoenicia it was who lent the colour, China the silken web and Hydaspes the weight of precious stones. Were you to have passed through the cities of Maeonia in this robe, Lydia would have handed over the thyrsus of vine-tendrils to you, Nysa performed her dances in your honour, the Bacchanals would have wondered to whom they owed their frenzy, the tigers meekly accepted your bonds. Just so does Liber, in fawnskin embroidered with Red Sea pearls, drive his chariot and guide the necks of Caspian tigers with ivory yoke: around him Satyrs and Maenads with streaming hair place chains of victorious ivy upon the Indians; Ganges, intoxicated, wears a wreath of his conqueror's vine-leaves.

Presently the joyful throne resounded with auspicious shout as your name is entered in the fasti for the fourth time. Liberty provides the annual spectacle of good omen; Law celebrates the custom derived from Vindex, and a slave, released from the bonds of his master, is led in and goes away a happier man because of the welcome blow. With a touch on his forehead the slave's unhappy state departs; the redness upon his cheeks has made him a citizen, and a lucky affront as his wish is granted has freed his back from the lash.

Hopes rise for good times to come for the Roman state in the year that bears your name. The evidence of your past performance gives confidence to those hopes: as often as your father appointed you to preside over the course of the year, so often he received fresh laurels. Once the Gruthungi broke down a forest, made themselves boats and dared to cross the Danube;

per fluvium plenae cuneis immanibus alni.   625
dux Odothaeus erat. tantae conamina classis
incipiens aetas et primus contudit annus:
summersae sedere rates; fluitantia numquam
largius Arctoos pavere cadavera pisces;
corporibus premitur Peuce; per quinque recurrens   630
ostia barbaricos vix egerit unda cruores,
confessusque parens Odothaei regis opima
rettulit exuviasque tibi. civile secundis
conficis auspiciis bellum. tibi debeat orbis
fata Gruthungorum debellatumque tyrannum.   635
Hister sanguineos egit te consule fluctus;
Alpinos genitor rupit te consule montes.
   Sed patriis olim fueras successibus auctor,
nunc eris ipse tuis. semper venere triumphi
cum trabeis sequiturque tuos victoria fasces.   640
sis, precor, adsiduus consul Mariique relinquas
et senis Augusti numerum. quae gaudia mundo,
per tua lanugo cum serpere coeperit ora,
cum tibi protulerit festas nox pronuba taedas!
quae tali devota toro, quae murice fulgens   645
ibit in amplexus tanti regina mariti?
quaenam tot divis veniet nurus, omnibus arvis
et toto donanda mari? quantusque feretur
idem per Zephyri metas Hymenaeus et Euri:
o mihi si liceat thalamis intendere carmen   650
conubiale tuis, si te iam dicere patrem!
tempus erit, cum tu trans Rheni cornua victor,
Arcadius captae spoliis Babylonis onustus
communem maiore toga signabitis annum,
crinitusque tuo sudabit fasce Suevus,   655
ultima fraternas horrebunt Bactra secures.

\

636-637 *verba* fluctus, Alpinos genitor rupit te consule *desunt in mss.*
restituit Bentinus in editione Isengrinii.   644 protulerit Emε *Isengr. mg.*,
prodiderit *cett.* 648 donanda: dotanda AP², dotata B. 655 Suevus AεEm,
lybeus Π¹, liebus Π²P¹, lieus B.

three thousand craft, laden with their savage freight, raced across the river. Odothaeus was their leader. The start of your life and your first year frustrated the attempt of that great fleet: its ships were swamped and sank; never did the fishes of the North gorge themselves more freely on floating corpses; Peuce is piled with bodies; the river flowed backwards, scarcely able to discharge the barbarian blood through its five mouths, and your father gave you the credit for the spoils of King Odothaeus and the booty. Under the auspices of your second consulship you put an end to civil war. Let the world acknowledge what it owes to you for the fate of the Gruthungi and the overthrow of a usurper. You were consul when the waves the Danube rolled were red with blood; you were consul when your father forced a way through the Alps.

But, once the author of your father's victories, now you will be the author of your own. Triumphs have ever marked your consulships and victory followed your axes. Be for ever consul, I pray, and surpass the record of Marius and Augustus in his old age. What joy for the world when the down begins to overspread your cheeks, and your wedding-night brings out the festive torches. What queen, pledged to such a couch, radiant in purple, will receive the embraces of so great a lord? Who will come as daughter by marriage to so many gods, to be dowered with every land and all the sea? What a shout of "Hymen" will be borne to the ends of West and East alike! O that it might be granted me to provide the wedding song for your nuptial bed, to hail you soon as a father! A time shall come when you, victor beyond the Rhine estuary, Arcadius, laden with the spoils of captive Babylon, will inscribe your shared year with a greater consulship, and beneath your rods the long-haired Swede will sweat, farthest Bactra tremble before your brother's axes.

COMMENTARY

I PROEM (προοίμιον). **1-17.** Another year opens under the auspices of an imperial consul. Behold the consular procession and how Bellona, discarding helmet and shield, carries the curule chair, and Gradivus, his breastplate replaced by the toga, bears the laurel-decked axes.

2. nota ... aula: because this is the fourth time that the consulship has come to Honorius, the child of a palace, not to speak of all the other times when the honour fell to an emperor.
iactantior: found in a similar context in Statius, *Silv.* 4.1.6f., the poem on the seventeenth consulship of Domitian. See on 655-656 below for a further echo of this poem.

5-17. A description of the *processus consularis* of Honorius. Ovid, *Ex Ponto* 4.4 and 4.9, refers to such a procession and Corippus, *In Laudem Iustini* 4.227ff., has a description of a later inauguration (A.D. 566), for which see Averil Cameron, *Corippus in Laudem Iustini* (London, 1976) *ad loc.* Claudian refers to other such *processus* at *Manl. Theod.* 276ff. and *Stil.* 2.396ff. (Full accounts of the ceremonial are to be found in R. Delbrueck, *Die Consulardiptychen und verwandte Denkmäler* I (Berlin-Leipsig 1929), and Daremberg-Saglio, *Dict. des Antiquités* (Paris, 1877) *art.* consul p.1472².)

5. armorum proceres legumque potentes: for details of the civil and military organization of the Empire at this period, see A.H.M. Jones, *Later Roman Empire* (Oxford, 1964) esp. Vol. 1, ch. 14; Vol. 2, chh. 15-17.

6. more Gabino: i.e. with one end of the toga girded closely around the body. The toga was worn in this fashion for ceremonies like the opening of the temple of Janus on the outbreak of war: see Virg. *Aen.* 7. 611 and Servius *ad loc.*, also R.M. Ogilvie, *Livy 1-5* (Oxford, 1965), p.731. Cf. *III Cons. Hon.* 3, *cinctus imitata Gabinos*, and *VI Cons. Hon.* 594, *habituque Gabino.*

7. discolor ... legio: because wearing the toga, not splendid uniform: cf. 9f., *togatus/miles*, and 568, *niveas ... cohortes.*

8. vexilla ...Quirini: the banners of the corporations (*collegia*).

11. Palatino ... senatu: the *comitatus*, the group of ministries attached to the emperor's person and forming the central government: see Jones *op.cit.* Vol. 1, pp.366ff. Members of this group were called *palatini.*

12. trabeam: the *trabea* is the consul's state robe of purple silk. Honorius' bejewelled *trabea* is described in 585ff.

12-13. Bellona .../sacras ... vectura curules: Claudian in his accounts of the *processus* tends to select bearers appropriate to the consul. Thus, Honorius is carried by Bellona, because of his alleged military prowess, while Gradivus (Mars) carries the fasces. Quirinus and Bellona perform a similar office for the warlike Stilicho (*Stil.* 2.370ff.). Theodorus, on the other hand, is attended by the Muses, as befits his scholarly disposition (*Manl. Theod.* 274ff.)

17. Eridani: the Padus (Po). Honorius entered upon his fourth consulship at Mediolanum, a name which Claudian avoids, though not from metrical considerations (cf. Ausonius, *Ord. Urb. Nob.* 7.1, *Et Mediolani mira omnia copia rerum*). At *Epith. Hon.* 182f. he uses a curious periphrasis for the city: *moenia Gallis/condita, lanigeri suis ostentia pellem*, an allusion to the supposed etymology of the name Mediolanum: cf. Isidore, *Orig.* 15.1, *vocatum Mediolanum ab eo, quod ibi sus in medio lanea perhibetur inventa.*

II RACE (γένος). 18-21. Descendant of the house of Trajan, yours is an old and warlike line. The might of your grandfather was felt by Britain and Africa, but his son, the emperor Theodosius, outstripped his fame. He stemmed the tide of barbarian invaders and propped up the tottering ruins of the Empire. Emperor of the East, he delivered the West from the tyrants Maximus and Arbogast. His anger never outlasted the day of battle and his mercy was freely extended to his defeated enemies. His generosity has secured the love and loyalty of his forces to his sons.

19. Ulpia progenies: Aurelius Victor (*Epit. de Caes.* 48.1) also traces the descent of the Theodosian house from Trajan, M. Ulpius Traianus. "The silence of Pacatus outweighs the venal evidence of Themistius, Victor and Claudian, who connect the family of Theodosius with the blood of Trajan and Hadrian." (Gibbon, ch. 26).

23. immenso . . . rerum de principe: cf. Virg. *Geo.* 4,382, *Oceanumque pater rerum.* The idea goes back to Homer, *Il.* 14.245-6, and represents an alternative cosmology to that described by Hesiod.

24. avus: the elder Theodosius, father of the Emperor, undertook important and successful military expeditions under Valentinian I: in Britain against the Picts and Scots (367-369, Ammianus 27.8.3); against the Alamanni (370, Amm. 28.5.15); and against Firmus, a Moorish chieftain who revolted against the corrupt and tyrannous Roman governor, Romanus (373, Amm. 29.5.4). Despite his distinguished services, he fell into disfavour and was beheaded at Carthage (376). Claudian omits the second of these campaigns, presumably to heighten the contrast between British North and African South. The African campaign is recalled in *Bell. Gild.* 325ff., where, appropriately, the elder Theodosius appears to Honorius in a dream and urges him to initiate action against Gildo in Africa.

31. maduerunt Saxone fuso: cf. Pacatus, *Paneg.* 5.2, *attritam pedestribus proeliis Britanniam referam? Saxo consumptus bellis navalibus offeretur*; and *Epith. Hon.* 219ff., *quidquid avus senior Mauro vel Saxone victis/. . . quaesivit.*

32. Orcades . . . Thyle: not mentioned in the accounts of Theodosius' exploits by Ammianus or Pacatus. Thyle or Thule (Norway? Iceland?) was first described by Pytheas: see *OCD*^{2} *s.v.* Thule.

33. Scottorum cumulos flevit glacialis Hiberne: the movement of the Scotti from their Irish home to the Welsh coast and Argyll began about the middle of the previous century. See R.G. Collingwood and J.N.L. Myers, *Roman Britain and the English Settlement*^{2} (Oxford, 1937) p.278.

34-35. per vasta cucurrit/Aethiopum cinxitque novis Atlanta maniplis: i.e. from the extreme East of Africa to the extreme West. The expedition seems to have embraced, in Claudian's account, as many points of interest, historical, literary and mythological, as the journey of Honorius related in *III Cons. Hon.*

36. virgineum Tritona: Triton is the name of a river and lake in N. Africa, mentioned as the birthplace of Athena (Apollodorus 1.4.6).

37. Gorgoneos . . . thalamos: the Gorgons dwelt on the farthest shore of Ocean, in the near neighbourhood of Night and the Hesperides (Hesiod *Theog.* 274ff.).

37-38. et vile virentes/Hesperidum risit, quos ditat fabula, ramos: for the golden apples of the Hesperides, daughters of Night, which Theodosius found to be green and common, see Hesiod *Theog.* 212f.

39. Iubae: Juba II and Bocchus (40) were kings of Mauretania in the first century B.C.

41-121. Claudian's account of the exploits of the Emperor Theodosius, called 'the Great'. He was born in Cilicia (345/6, Aurelius Victor 48.19) and, as *dux Moesiae primae*, while still a young man, defeated the Sarmatians and called a halt to the advance of the northern tribes then pouring over Pannonia (373, Ammianus 29.6.15). He lived in retirement in Spain following his father's death, whence Gratian, unable to cope with the barbarian menace after the death of Valens at Adrianople, 378, called him to be emperor of the East. He was proclaimed at Sirmium in 379. Illyricum, hitherto administered by the West, was partitioned and its eastern dioceses of Dacia and Macedonia placed under the rule of Theodosius. Stein, *loc.cit.* 1 p.191 and note 5.

47. digna legi virtus: cf. Pacatus 7.1, *virtus tua meruit imperium.*

49-50. gementem . . . Rhodopen: Rhodope, mt. of Thrace. Zosimus (4.24. 4) mentions the presence of the Goths in large numbers in Thrace, Moesia and Pannonia, at the time of Theodosius' accession. The names *Mysia* and *Moesia* are often confused: Birt proposed *Moesia* at 53 against the mss.

53. plaustris: wagons naturally form part of the equipment of a migrant race, and Zosimus (4.25.3) relates how no fewer than 4,000 of them were captured on this occasion.

54. flavaque . . . agmina: cf. *Rapt. Pros.* 2.65, *flavos . . . Getas.*
Bistonios . . . campos: Thrace.

62-69. An elaborate comparison (σύγκρισις) rounds off the passage. These comparisons are an important feature of panegyric: see Menander Rhet. (L. Spengel, *Rhetores Graeci*, Leipsig, 1853-56, vol. 3, p.376). The Phaethon story is a particular favourite of Claudian: *P.O.* 258; *III Cons. Hon.* 124; *Ruf.* 2.211; *VI Cons. Hon.* 187-90; *Rapt. Pros.* 3.403; *c.m.* 44.107.

69-97. Claudian's account of how Theodosius, emperor of the East, rid the West of the pretenders Maximus and Eugenius and, incidentally, completed the transfer of power in the West from the dynasty of Valentinian to his own. As in his account of the elder Theodosius (24-40), Claudian relies heavily on antithesis in relating how the Emperor dealt with these two rebellions. Maximus was headlong and impetuous: Arbogast cautious.

Maximus deployed his troops: Arbogast closed his ranks. But in their origins and their ends both were equal.

70-71. at non pars altera rerum/tradita: this part of the story might be fitly entitled "How the West was Won". The death of Valentinian I in 375 left Valens on the throne of the East, while the West was ruled jointly by Gratian, who held Gaul, Spain and Britain, and Valentinian II, who ruled Italy, Illyricum and Africa under the regency of his mother Justina. When Valens perished at the battle of Adrianople, 378, he was succeeded the following year by Theodosius, the last Westerner to be emperor of the East. The removal of Gratian (see note on 73) and Valentinian II (see note on 74) and the defeat of the usurpers Maximus and Eugenius left Theodosius in control of both *partes imperii*.

72. gemini . . . tyranni: Maximus and Eugenius.

73. hunc saeva Britannia fudit: the revolt of Magnus Maximus, a Spaniard, began in Britain in 383, where he was acclaimed Augustus by the army. On his entering Gaul most of Gratian's army defected to him. Gratian attempted to take refuge in Gaul but was intercepted, held for a time at Lugdunum, then assassinated. See note on 91-92. Theodosius acquiesced in the usurper's role until 388, by which time Maximus had penetrated into Western Illyricum. He was defeated by Theodosius at the battle of Aquileia and massacred by the victorious Theodosians, 28 August 388.

74. hunc simul Germanus famulum delegerat exul: the *Germanus exul* is Arbogast, a Frankish soldier whom Theodosius had employed as *magister militum* to eradicate the remnants of Maximus' followers in Gaul. On the death of Justina, Theodosius, who in 387 had married Galla, the sister of Valentinian II, sent the young emperor to Vienne under the protection of Arbogast. The *famulus* is Flavius Eugenius, a former teacher of rhetoric and *magister scriniorum*, whom Arbogast set up as emperor when Valentinian was strangled in his palace in 392. A point of some significance about the threat posed by the usurpers is that, in view of Theodosius' strong line against paganism, Arbogast provided a focus or hope for the pagan senatorial body in the West. In 394 Theodosius eventually moved against Eugenius and Arbogast and defeated them at the battle of the Frigidus (Wippach, Vipacco). It is interesting to note that Stilicho held a subordinate command in Theodosius' main force (Zosimus 4.57) and the Visigoth Alaric was amongst the barbarian auxiliaries (Socrates 7.10).

77. dabant: see note on 262-263.

91-92. amborum periere duces: hic sponte carina/decidit in fluctus, illum suus abstulit ensis: Andragathius was the *magister equitum* of Maximus, and it was he who was conveyed into Gratian's presence in a litter thought to contain the Empress in order to assassinate him. At Aquileia he leapt from his ship and was drowned (Sozomen 7.13-14; Zosimus 4.47.1). Arbogast after the death of Eugenius fled to the Alps and committed suicide (Zosimus 4.58.6).

93-97. Claudian typically and effortlessly rings the changes on the same theme — the vengeance taken for the murder of the imperial brothers — no fewer than five times.

96. has dedit inferias tumulis: cf. Ovid *Fasti* 5.422, *tumulo . . . inferias dederat.*
inferiae: sacrifices paid to the dead.

101. nuntius ipse sui: Zosimus (4.58.1) confirms this tribute to Theo-dosius' speed: τῆς διὰ τῶν Ἄλπεων παρόδου κρατήσας παρὰ πᾶσαν ἐλπίδα τοῖς πολεμίοις ἐπέστη. ("He secured a passage over the Alps and con-fronted the enemy against all expectation.")

104-109. extruite immanes scopulos . . . qui vindicet, ibit: Claudian's audience could hardly have failed to see in this highly moralizing colophon to the story of Maximus and Eugenius a reference to the punishment that awaited the rebellious Gildo. Döpp, *loc.cit.* p.123, draws attention to a more definite coupling of Gildo with the pretenders that Theodosius routed in *Bell. Gild.* 5-6: *patriis solum quod defuit armis,/tertius occubuit nati (sc. Honorii) virtute tyrannus.*

113. mitis precibus: this tribute to Theodosius' leniency after the defeat of Eugenius is echoed by Zosimus (4.58). Ambrose, *De obitu Theodosii,* describes him as one *qui numquam veniam petenti negaret.* The massacre he ordered at Thessalonica in 390 and for which Ambrose caused him to do penance reveals a harsher side to his nature.

121. hinc natis mansura fides: similarly Ambrose, *De obitu Theod.* 2, *non sunt destituti quibus . . . Theodosius acquisivit . . . et exercitus fidem.*

III BIRTH (γένεσις). 121-158. Majesty was yours from birth. Your in-fant form, wrapped in the purple, was laid upon a royal breast. Spain was your father's birthplace, the Bosporus yours: East and West claim you as their own. Not for you the narrow shores and bleak rocks that witnessed the birth of Hercules and Bacchus, Apollo and Jupiter. You, born on a bed of purple amid portents of good omen, gave your name to the year of your birth.

121-127. Honorius enjoyed the distinction of being born the child of an emperor, a distinction not shared by his brother, Arcadius, who was born 377/8, before Theodosius became emperor in 379: hence, *te regia solum/ protulit* (124-25). He was born in Constantinople: for the date see note on 153-158. The word *ortu* (121) is more grandiloquent than might appear. Here it must mean 'origins' or 'antecedents', but at this period it could mean 'accession' (*Cod. Theod.* [389] 2.8.19.4) and carried suggestions of imperial sun-imagery: see E.H. Kantorowicz, 'Oriens Augusti – lever du Soleil', *Dumbarton Oaks Papers,* 17 (1963) 119ff. According to Menander (*R.G.* 3,271) the next section (ἀνατροφή) is the proper place for the topic treated here in 121-127.

132-138. These lines contain an unmistakable rephrasing of Pacatus' Pane-gyric on Theodosius, 4: *cedat his terris terra Cretensis parvi Iovis gloriata cunabulis et geminis Delos reptata numinibus et alumno Hercule nobiles Thebae.*

132. Thebas: Thebes was the birthplace of Hercules and Bacchus (Bromius).

133. haesit . . . Delos: Latona gave birth to Apollo at Mt. Cynthus in Delos, which, according to legend, was a floating island. After his birth it ceased to be unstable (ἄδηλος) and became Delos: cf. Stat. *Ach.* 1.388, *instabili Delo*, and *P.O.* 185, *ad loca nutricis iam non errantia Deli*. For the story, see Callimachus, *Hymnus in Delon*, 28-54.

134-135. Cretaque ... Dictaeis: the birthplace of Jupiter was a cave on Mt. Dicte in Crete. For the participle *reptata* cf. Pacatus *loc.cit.* above.

139. Honorius' mother was Aelia Flaccilla (*Laus Serenae* 69) or Placilla (Socrates 5.12). She died *ca* 386, having borne Theodosius two other children, Arcadius and Pulcheria. Gregory of Nyssa composed her funeral oration. Theodosius later married Galla, the sister of Valentinian II, but was widowed again in 394 just before the campaign against Eugenius and Arbogast. Galla Placidia was a child of this second marriage.

140-141. ululata verendis/aula puerperiis: i.e., the palace resounded with the cries of Flaccilla in labour: cf. Stat. *Theb.* 3.158, *nulloque ululata dolore ... Lucina.*

142. quae voces avium? quanti per inane volatus?: Servius *ad Virg. Aen.* 3.361: *aves aut oscines sunt aut praepetes: oscines quae ore futura praedicant; praepetes quae volatu augurium significant.* The re-awakening of oracles long silent and the prophetic activities that Claudian describes here are not to be taken seriously. He is merely using a recommended topos of the genre (Menander *R.G.* 3.371).

143. corniger Hammon: the Egyptian Zeus, whose oracle at Siwa was no less celebrated than Delphi or Dodona. He was represented as having ram's horns, hence *corniger Hammon*: cf. Ovid *A.A.* 3.789; *Met.* 5.18.

145-147. Persae ... Etruscus ... Babylonius ... Chaldaei: all anciently famed for their skill in the various branches of soothsaying and divination.

147-148. Cumanaque rursus/intonuit rupes, rabidae delubra Sibyllae: the seat of the Sibyl was at Cumae. A collection of her utterances was deposited in the Capitol and solemnly consulted in times of national difficulty. When this collection was destroyed in the burning of the Capitol in 83 B.C., a new collection was made, which was consulted as late as 363 (Amm. Marc. 23.1.7). A few years after Claudian wrote these lines, his hero Stilicho ordered the destruction of the Sibylline Books (Rutilius Namatianus 2.52). **rabidae:** cf. Virgil's account of her frenzy (*Aen.* 6.77ff.): *tanto magis ille fatigat/os rabidum* (79-80).

149-150. nec te progenitum Cybeleius aere sonoro/lustravit Corybas: the Corybants were the attendants of the Phrygian goddess Cybĕle, or Cybēbe, who came to be identified with Rhea, the mother of Zeus. To protect him from his father Cronos, his cries were drowned by the armed dance of the Cretan Curetes, in which they clashed their arms together. For a similar association of Corybantes and Curetes in the birth of Zeus, cf. Ovid *Fasti* 4.209f.: *pars clipeos sudibus, galeas pars tundit inanes:/hoc Curetes habent, hoc Corybantes opus.*

150. exercitus undique fulgens/adstitit: cf. *III Cons. Hon.* 14, *lustravitque ... tuos ... ortus miles.*

154-158. A typical piece of panegyrical licence. The date of Honorius' birth was 9 September in the consulship of Richomer and Clearchus, i.e. 384 (Socrates 5.12). The year 384 is also given in the chronicles of Idatius and Marcellinus. Of this date Claudian was in no doubt, and confirms it by telling us that when Theodosius was setting out against Eugenius in 394, Honorius was not quite ten: *necdum decimas emensus aristas* (372). It was not until 386 that Honorius had his first consulship, and the passage is a piece of mild deception to enhance encomiastic effect.

157. Quirinali . . . amictu: the consular *trabea*: cf. Virg. *Aen.* 7.612, *Quirinali trabea*, and *In Eutr.* 1.28, *Quirinales . . . cinctus.*

IV EDUCATION (ἀνατροφή). 159-427.

(a) 159-211. You were suckled at the breasts of goddesses. Diana trained you for the hunt: Pallas for the arts of war. Soon you were made Augustus, while Heaven beamed approval.

This is an unusually extended treatment of this section, a circumstance probably to be attributed to the fact that Honorius' youth — he was in his fourteenth year — and the paucity of his achievements did not provide Claudian with much material for what would normally be the main section, exploits. The last two lines of the previous section (157-158) might equally well be included under the heading of ἀνατροφή. I leave them under γένεσις, because of their reference to the idea of Honorius' first consulship allegedly occurring in the year of his birth. At all events, the transition between the two sections is nicely managed.

161. Maenalios arcus: Maenalus, a mountain in Arcadia, was one of the haunts of Diana: cf. Stat. *Theb.* 12.125, *Maenaliae . . . Dianae*. For Honorius' prowess in the hunt, see *Fesc.* 1.10-15.

165-166. saepe tuas etiam iam tum gaudente marito/velavit regina comas: *sc. diademata* (167); *etiam*, because Arcadius was already Augustus.

166. festinaque voti: "anticipating her wish": the same expression occurs at Stat. *Theb.* 6.75, *festinus voti pater.*

169-170. mutatur principe Caesar;/ protinus aequaris fratri: Honorius became Augustus in 393; Arcadius had been elevated in 383. The Ravenna Chronicle gives the date of Honorius' elevation at Constantinople as 23 January 393. But Socrates (5.25) says ἐν τῇ ἑαυτοῦ τρίτῃ ὑπατείᾳ καὶ Ἀβουνδαντίου τῇ δεκάτῃ τοῦ Ἰαννουαρίου μηνός, i.e. 10 January, in the third consulship of Theodosius and the consulship of Abundantius (393). Socrates (*loc.cit.*), Sozomen (7.24), Philostorgius (11.2) and even Claudian make Theodosius' expedition against Eugenius (394) follow hard on this event. The movements of Theodosius may be traced through the *Codex Theodosianus* and there is no evidence of his having left Constantinople before 394. Socrates' date of 10 January 393 may well be right, for in *Codex Theodosianus* the enactment 1.7.2, *de officio magistri militum*, is dated *Constantinopoli, ii Id.Ian. Theodosio A. III et Abundantio coss.*, and is headed *Imppp. Theodosius Arcadius et Honorius AAA.*

170-173. non certius umquam/hortati superi, nulli praesentior aether/ adfuit ominibus: the omen Claudian describes is recorded by the Ravenna Chronicle *a. 393, tenebrae factae sunt die solis hora iii, vi Kal. Nov.* It is not there linked with the elevation of Honorius as in Claudian and in the Chronicle of Marcellinus. Claudian's description does not suggest an eclipse.

174. cum solita miles te voce levasset: a reference to the elevation of the new Augustus on a shield by the soldiers and their hailing him as emperor. Cf. Zosimus 3.92 (of the emperor Julian): καὶ ἐπί τινος ἀσπίδος μετέωρον ἄραντες ἀνεῖπόν τε σεβαστὸν αὐτοκράτορα καὶ ἐπέθεσαν σὺν βίᾳ τὸ διάδημα τῇ κεφαλῇ ("and raising him aloft on a shield they saluted him as Augustus Emperor and roughly placed the crown on his head").

179. Pangaea (n. pl.): mountain in Thrace.

180. palus Maeotia: the Sea of Azov, often called *palus* because of its shallowness.

182-183. imperii lux illa fuit . . . risitque tuo natura sereno: cf. *VI Cons. Hon.* 537ff.:

> ipse favens votis solitoque decentior aer,
> quamvis assiduo noctem foedaverat imbre,
> principis et solis radiis detersa removit
> nubila . . .

184-185. audax/stella: a second omen, a new bright star, seen in daylight, therefore bold: cf. 186-87, *alieni temporis hospes/ignis.*

186. quantus numeratur nocte Bootes: the Bearward is regarded as a constellation, not a single star: hence *numeratur.*

189. parens Augusta: Flaccilla died *ca* 386, see note on 139.

190. divi sidus avi: the elder Theodosius (died 376): see note on 24. The epithet *divus* is normally applied to a deceased emperor. Here, however, it is the father of the emperor who is so described. It is applied to the elder Theodosius in *CIL* vi 1730 where Stilicho is described as *progenero divi Theodosii*. Since *progener* means 'husband of a granddaughter', and since Stilicho stood in that relationship to the elder Theodosius and not the emperor, to whom he would be *gener*, it would seem that Claudian is using the epithet *divus* advisedly. See Cameron, *Claudian* (Oxford, 1970) p.57.

192-195. ventura potestas/claruit Ascanio . . . tempora candor: these lines refer to the story of the fire that wreathed the head of Aeneas' son, Ascanius, told by Virgil, *Aen.* 2.682ff. A similar re-working of the Virgilian omen occurs in Sil. Ital. 16.119ff. in regard to Masinissa. The implication is that the omens that attended Honorius' elevation were of an even higher order, since the fires involved were in the heavens (196).

197-202. talis ab Idaeis . . . lacerto: now Honorius is compared with the infant Jupiter in the caves of Crete (*Idaeis . . . antris*). Claudian tends to intersperse his comparisons thtoughout the work, instead of making a separate section: see note on 62-69.

201. moturae convexa comae: the idea goes back to Homer, *Il.* 1.529f.; cf. also Ovid, *Met.* 1.179f.: *terrificam capitis concussit terque quaterque/ caesariem, cum qua terram, mare, sidera movit.*

204. redibat: i.e. from the place where Honorius was made Augustus, *viz.* the seventh milestone from the city of Constantinople (Marcellinus *Chron. a.* 393).

206-211. The scene is embellished by a further comparison, this time of Theodosius, Arcadius and Honorius with the Spartan twins (*gemini . . . Lacones,* 206) Castor and Pollux, and their father Jupiter. Their mother was Leda (207) and the sister is Helen.

207-208. in utroque relucet/frater, utroque soror: an echo of Martial 9.103.4, *atque in utroque nitet Tyndaris ore soror.*

209. stellati pariter crines: the light that appeared on the heads of Castor and Pollux during the expedition of the Argo for the reassurance of mariners (*miseris olim plorabile nautis*, Val. Flacc. 1.573), later called St. Elmo's fire, is described as stars by Diodorus Siculus 4.43.2 and Seneca *Nat. Quaest.* 1.1.13. The device of the star-crowned twins was long in use on the reverse of the Roman denarius.

(b) 214-418. Theodosius addresses Honorius on the duties of a prince.

On the sources of the speech (which, of course, is probably in no way indebted to Theodosius) see T. Birt, *De fide Christiana quantum Stilichonis aetate in aula imperatoria occidentali valuerit* (Marburg, 1885), who there argues that Claudian has drawn on Synesius' *De Regno*, which was addressed to Arcadius at a date near enough to *IV Cons. Hon.* in point of time to prompt the question, Did Claudian imitate Synesius or *vice versa*? Birt sets forth the parallels and concludes that Synesius was Claudian's model. A similar line is taken by O. Kehding (*De panegyricis latinis capita quattuor*, Marburg, 1899). The *De Regno* of Synesius is now regarded as a later composition than *IV Cons. Hon.*, and any resemblances between the two are to be explained by the fact that both writers had the same access to all that had been written on this commonplace theme. See Cameron, *Claudian*, pp.321f.

214-216. Parthorum ... Arsacio: the Arsacids were the royal dynasty of Parthia, from the mid-third century B.C. until the middle of the third century A.D., when Persia shook off their suzerainty. Arsaces was the founder of the dynasty. The names *Parthi* and *Persae* are used indifferently by the Roman poets: see Nisbet-Hubbard on Horace *Odes* 1.2.22. At *In Eutr.* 1.414ff., Claudian makes the goddess Roma speak of the Parthians and the Arsacids with the same contempt. Theodosius had succeeded in effecting a settlement with Persia (387): see E. Stein, *Histoire du Bas-Empire*, vol. 1 pp.205f. (Bruges, 1959) and *Stil.* 1.51ff.

219-220. altera Romanae longe rectoribus aulae/condicio: Claudian, by hindsight, represents Theodosius as earmarking the Western empire for his younger son. The death of Theodosius on 17 January 395 left Arcadius as ruler of the Eastern Empire, and Honorius as ruler of the West. One is left at this point with the feeling that the qualities required of an Eastern potentate like Arcadius are of an inferior order to those required in the West.

220. virtute decet, non sanguine niti: cf. Juvenal 8, *init.: stemmata quid faciunt, quid prodest, Pontice, longo/sanguine censeri ... si ... male vivitur.*

222. vile latens virtus: Pacatus in his panegyric on Theodosius (17.5) has: *sibi humilitatem et tenebras suas imputet iacens virtus quae non obtulit se probandam.* Similarly Boethius *Consol.* 1.5.34f., *latet obscuris condita virtus/clara tenebris.*

223. sine remige puppis: cf. Archpoet 10.9, *feror ego veluti sine nauta navis.*

225-227. hanc tamen haud quisquam, qui non agnoverit ante/semet ... inveniet: *hanc:* sc. *virtutem.* The importance of self-knowledge goes back to the famous inscription on the temple at Delphi, ΓΝΩΘΙ ΣΕΑΥΤΟΝ. Cicero singles it out as one of the areas of agreement between the Stoics and other schools of philosophy (*de Fin.* 4.25). On Claudian's knowledge of philosophy, see Cameron *loc.cit.* pp.323ff.

228-254. Claudian here combines the myth of the creation of mortals by Prometheus (Plato *Protagoras* 320D ff.) and the Platonic theory of the tripartite division of the soul (*Republic* 4.439D ff. and 9.580D ff.; *Timaeus* 69C ff.). The soul has three divisions: τὸ λογιστικόν (τὸ μὲν ᾧ μανθάνει ἄνθρωπος, *mens*); τὸ θυμοειδές (τὸ ᾧ θυμοῦται, *ira*); τὸ ἐπιθυμητικόν, *cupido*). Reason was placed in the head and the other two parts, anger and desire, in the trunk. Cicero *Tusc.* 1.20: *Plato triplicem finxit animum, cuius principatum, id est rationem, in capite sicut in arce posuit, et duas partes parere voluit, iram et cupiditatem, quas locis disclusit: iram in pectore, cupiditatem supter praecordia locavit.* Cf. also Horace *Odes* 1.16.13ff. and Nisbet-Hubbard *ad loc.*

229. aetheriis miscens terrena: *aetheriis*, the artistic skill and fire stolen from Athena and Hephaestus (Plato *Progatoras loc.cit.*) and *ratio* (*sinceram ... mentem*, 230). *terrena*, the clay from which man was formed (*principi limo*, Horace *loc.cit.*).

233. geminas: i.e. *ira* and *cupido*.

234-235. haec ... hanc: i.e. *ratio, mens.*

235. alta capitis ... in arce: similarly Cic. *Tusc.* 1.20 (quoted above). Cf. Archpoet 4.59, *dum in arce cerebri Bacchus dominatur.*

236. mandatricem operum prospecturamque labori: "to govern its functions and to oversee the work". This is the only occurrence of *mandatrix* cited by *Thes. Ling. Lat.*

237-238. praeceptaque summae/passuras dominae: cf. Cicero *loc.cit., et duas partes parere (sc. rationi) voluit.*

239. veritus confundere sacra profanis: Plato *Tim. loc.cit.*, σεβόμενοι μιαίνειν τὸ θεῖον ... ("fearing to pollute the divine ...").

246. invenit pulmonis opem: Plato *Tim.* 70C, ἐπικουρίαν αὐτῇ μηχανώμενοι τὴν τοῦ πλεύμονος ἰδέαν ἐνεφύτευσαν ... ἵνα τό τε πνεῦμα καὶ τὸ πῶμα δεχομένη, ψύχουσα, ἀναπνοὴν καὶ ῥᾳστώνην ἐν τῷ καύματι παρέχοι ("by way of relief, they contrived and implanted the form of the lung ... in order that it, receiving breath and drink, might have a cooling effect and provide recovery and ease amidst the heat").

256. dabit purae sacraria mentis: Mens or Mens Bona was worshipped at Rome as a goddess, with a temple on the Capitol. This line is virtually an inversion of a Propertian idea: *Mens Bona, si qua dea es, tua me in sacraria dono* (3.24.19).

258. Serēs: the Chinese.

261-262. tunc omnia iure tenebis/cum poteris rex esse tui: Synesius gives the same counsel to Arcadius (*De Regno* 10): φημὶ δεῖ ... τὸν βασιλέα πρῶτον αὐτὸν αὐτοῦ βασιλέα εἶναι.

262-263. proclivior usus/in peiora datur: *sc. usus fit proclivior in peiora,* "the practice of vice tends to worse vices". For this use of *do = facio,* cf. 77, *cautumque dabant exempla sequentem.*

270-275. For the sentiment, compare Seneca *De Clem.* 1.8.1, *tibi non magis quam soli latere contingit;* Pliny *Pan.* 83.1, *habet hoc primum magna fortuna, quod nihil tectum, nihil occultum esse patitur.*

270. medio ... in ore: "in full view"; cf. Cic. *Verr. act. sec.* 2.81: *quae in ore atque in oculis provinciae gesta sunt.*

273. lux altissima fati: by hypallage for *lux altissimi fati.* For the "light" of a consul, cf. Statius *Silv.* 4.1.26, *lucemque a consule ducit/omnis honos.*

278. suspectus: the participle may be taken as active, like *cautus, consideratus* etc.

281-282. non sic excubiae, non circumstantia pila/quam tutatur amor: a well-worn commonplace: cf. Cic. *Phil.* 2.112, *caritate te et benevolentia civium saeptum oportet esse.* The combination of *sic ... quam,* used again at 300-301 below, is not particularly common, but cf. Prop. 2.9.3ff.

284-286. Kehding (*loc.cit.*) traces this comparison between cosmic and civic harmony back to Aelius Aristeides, περὶ ὁμονοίας ταῖς πόλεσιν (794 Dindorf). Cf. especially τὸν πάντα οὐρανὸν καὶ κόσμον ... μία δήπου γνώμη καὶ φιλίας δύναμις διοικεῖ ("one sentiment and the power of love rule the whole heaven and the universe").

286-289. The celebrated opening of *In Ruf.* 1 includes a similar view of cosmic order.

286-287. limite ... medio: "The sun is content with the limits of the torrid zone." W.H. Semple, 'Some Astronomical Passages in Claudian', *CQ* 33, 1939, pp.1ff. Cf. *In Ruf.* 2.210f.: *limite iusto/devius ... Phaethon.*

290. qui terret plus ipse timet: Seneca *De Ira* 2.11.3, *necesse est multos timeat quem multi timent:* a very tired commonplace.

296-302. The importance of princely example is another commonplace. Cf. (*inter alia*) Pacatus 14.4, *exasperat homines imperata correctio, blandissime iubetur exemplo;* Symmachus *Epp.* 2,13, *augustius est regenti sibi quam subditis modum ponere.*

306-311. Claudian stresses, as he did at the outset of this section, that Honorius is to rule Romans, not decadent Easterns.

306. Sabaeos: a people of Arabia Felix; cf. 258, *mollis Arabs.*

308. Assyriam, tenuit quam femina, gentem: he means Semiramis, the foundress of Babylon, whose second husband was Ninus, King of Assyria.

314. rupes Caprearum taetra: where Tiberius spent the last eleven years of his life (26-37 A.D.). Claudian uses a similar periphrasis for Tiberius at *In Eutr.* 2.61, *senis infandi Capreae,* where he is also coupled with Nero.

316. gloria Traiani: for the connection between the Theodosian dynasty and Trajan, see 19 and note.

317. triumphati ... Parthi: for Trajan's campaigns in the East, 113-117, see Dio Cassius 68.17-32. For the passive use of *triumphare,* cf. *III Cons. Hon.* 25, *triumphato ... ab Histro.*

318. fractis ... Dacis: Trajan celebrated triumphs for two campaigns against Decebalus, the Dacian king, 101-2 and 105-6: Dio Cassius 68.6ff. Pliny (to Caninius about to write a history of the Dacian Wars) *Epp.* 8.4.1: *dices ... super haec actos bis triumphos, quorum alter ex invicta gente primus, alter novissimus fuit.* Claudian *VI Cons. Hon.* 335, *Dacia belli-potens cum fregerat Ulpius arma.*

alta ... invectus ... Capitolia: for the accusative without preposition, cf. Virg. *Aen.* 8.714f., *Caesar triplici invectus Romana triumpho/moenia.*

320-352. Theodosius impresses on his son the importance of the martial arts.

321. si bella canant: a difficult phrase, perhaps explained by Claudian's figurative use of *classica = bella* at 25.

322. segnes: proleptically with *manus.*

329. tum tibi murali libretur machina pulsu: "then swing your catapult into action against the walls". Claudian is thinking perhaps of Virgil, *Aen.* 12.921f., *murali concita numquam/tormento sic saxa fremunt.* The *machina* is, of course, the *tormentum* or *ballista.* For fuller details of this and the other engines of war here mentioned, *aries* (330), *testudo* (331), see E.W. Marsden, *Greek and Roman Artillery: Historical Development* (Oxford, 1969), index *s.vv.* "catapults", "rams, battering", "tortoises, siege-sheds".

331-332. ruat emersura iuventus/effusi per operta soli: the walls of cities under siege were sometimes penetrated by an underground tunnel (*cuni-culus*), as in Camillus' capture of Veii in 396 B.C. (Livy 5.19ff.).

337-338. neu tibi regificis tentoria larga redundent/deliciis: if Claudian had wished to add an *exemplum* of *luxuries armata*, he might have alluded to Otho (Tacitus *Hist.* 2), censured by Juvenal for this failing at *Sat.* 2.102ff.

345. sumpta ne pudeat quercum stravisse bipenni: like Caesar in Lucan 3.433f., *primus raptam vibrare bipennem/ausus.*

(c) **353-369.** Honorius interrupts his father with the request to be allowed to put all this good advice into practice by joining him in the campaign against Eugenius.

The content of these lines is more akin to ἐπιτηδεύματα, (youthful pursuits and predilections as evidence of character), which in the scheme for panegyrics proposed by Menander is a separate section following ἀνατροφή (*R.G.* 3.368ff.). Claudian's procedure here, in working ἐπιτηδεύματα into the section on ἀνατροφή, is more in keeping with Aphthonius' scheme (*R.G.* 2.36ff.).

354. haec effecta dabo: *haec efficiam;* see note on 262-263.

357. gelidas nunc tendis in Alpes: Claudian avails himself of a panegyrist's licence to bring separated events closer together. See note on 169-170.

358-359. tyrannum ... barbarus: the tyrant is Eugenius; the *barbarus,* Arbogast (cf. *III Cons. Hon.* 66, *barbarus ... exul,* and 74 above, *Ger-manus exul*).

361. patiar Romam servire clienti?: *sc. Eugenio;* similarly *III Cons. Hon.* 67, *sceptraque deiecto dederat Romana clienti.*

363. cognati . . . cruoris: i.e. of Valentinian II: see notes on 74 and 139.
366. solus: because Troy could not be taken without the presence of Pyrrhus: Soph. *Philoct.* 114ff.

(d) 369-395. Theodosius checks Honorius' youthful ardour, and, as though with a premonition of his death, urges him to continue his preparation for the task that will devolve on him and his brother.

374. Pellaeus: i.e. Alexander, so called from Pella, the Macedonian capital. For his conquest of Porus at the Hydaspes, see Quintus Curtius 8.12f.
376-377. flevisse . . . nil sibi vincendum . . . relinqui: cf. Juvenal 10.168f., *unus Pellaeo iuveni non sufficit orbis,/aestuat infelix angusto limite mundi.*
378. promittere: "foretell". The word seems to have belonged to augural language: see Cicero, *ad Fam.* 6.1.5.
380-382. sic . . . stridula . . . examina regem nascentem venerantur apes: Xenophon, *Cyrop.* 5.1.24, draws a similar comparison to which the present passage is heavily indebted. The ancients of course regarded the queen bee as a male (Virg. *Geo.* 4.210), though Xenophon once speaks of ἡ ἐν τῷ σμήνει ἡγεμὼν μέλιττα (*Oec.* 7.17).
390. si pateant Alpes: cf. *clausos montes*, 103 above, and *Bell. Get.* 471, *post Alpes . . . apertas.* The Julian Alps were the scene of the overthrow of Arbogast and Eugenius.
391-392. aderis, partesque receptas/suscipies: for Theodosius' redemption of this promise, see *III Cons. Hon.* 105ff. That and the present passage tell against Zosimus' statement (4.58) that Honorius accompanied his father on this campaign. Here, as at 582ff., only Gaul (392) and Spain (393) are mentioned as areas belonging to Honorius' rule. The omission of Africa is significant and relevant both to the dramatic date of this passage (the eve of the campaign against Eugenius, 394) and to the situation prevailing at the date of composition (end of 397). On both occasions Africa was under a cloud. In 394 Gildo had maintained a position of neutrality and provided no assistance for Theodosius in the expedition against Eugenius (*Bell. Gild.* 1.246ff., *VI Cons. Hon.* 108ff.). By the beginning of winter, 397, Gildo had been declared *hostis publicus* by Rome: *veniens indixit hiems . . . hostem* (*Bell. Gild.* 16). See further on 436-438 below.

(e) 396-427. Theodosius impressed on Honorius the importance of the study of history and particularly recommends the examples of the heroes of Republican Rome. The section ends with a graceful simile of an old mariner instructing his son in the principles of seamanship.

397. quae mox imitere legat: Roman moralists relied heavily on the force of example. Horace's father is a case in point (*Serm.* 1.4.105ff.) though, as an unlettered ex-slave, he found his *exempla* among living contemporaries. Under the Empire, a large fund of historical *exempla* was made available to rhetoricians and moralists in works like Valerius Maximus *De factis dictisque memorabilibus.* On Claudian's knowledge and use of such *exempla*, see now Cameron, *loc.cit.* pp.336-343, especially 338f.

397-398. nec desinat umquam/tecum Graia loqui, tecum Romana vetustas:
cf. *Epith.* 232, [*Maria*] *Latios nec volvere libros/desinit aut Graios*, and
P.O. 198, *Graeca vetustas*.

400. Latium retro te confer in aevum: satirists and moralists of the Empire
show a distinct preference for the old Republican days, which for them
had taken on the aspect of a Golden Age, with which they constantly
contrasted the corruption of their own times. See H.W. Litchfield,
'National *Exempla Virtutis* in Roman Literature', *Harvard Studies in
Classical Philology*, 25 (1914) pp.1-71, esp. pp.53-59, for this tendency to
restrict the range of eligible *exempla* to the republican period.

400-418. The stories of the people here listed as *exempla* of the particular
qualities attached to their names will be found in any Classical Dictionary.
An equally elaborate list of Roman worthies occurs at *In Eutr.* 1.439ff.,
and is used there to point up the contrast between their labours and
sacrifices and the excesses of the eunuch consul Eutropius.

402-403. Metti ... Torquati: these two stand together as *exempla* of
qualities to be avoided. The punishment of the former is mentioned again
at *Bell. Gild.* 254: Cicero in *Pro Sulla* 32 takes a more lenient view of the
rigor nimius of the latter.

411. adversa Catonis: "The failure of Cato is greater than any success."
His death at Utica in 46 B.C. made him a more formidable opponent than
he had been in life.

412-418. Claudian turns from *exempla* of heroism to three *exempla* of
paupertas sobria used in a similar context in *In Ruf.* 1.200-203.

416-417. fascesque salignis/postibus adfixi: not so long before (3-4),
Claudian was telling us how splendid it is that the fasces have been re-
moved from the doors of mere commoners!

416-418. lictore ... consule ... colono: the ablative without *ab* is not
uncommon in verse; cf. Juv. 1.13, *ruptae lectore columnae*, etc.

418. trabeato ... colono: the *trabea* is at this time as much a symbol of
the consulship as the fasces formerly were.

422. aequoreas alni nato commendat habenas: the idea of the ship as the
chariot of the sea is common in Greek and Latin poetry; cf. Catullus 64.9,
volitantem flamine currum, and Virgil *Aen.* 6.1, *classique inmittit habenas*.
alni: the alder, like the pine, was commonly used in shipbuilding; cf. Virg.
Geo. 1.136, *alnos ... cavatas*.

425. fraus infida sereni: cf. Virg. *Aen.* 5.851, *caeli totiens deceptus fraude
sereni*, and *Geo.* 1.426 (to which passage Claudian is much indebted for
this and the other pieces of weather-lore here given), *insidiis noctis capiere
serenae*.

426-427. quo saucia vento/decolor iratos attollat Cynthia vultus: Virg.
Geo. 1.430f., *at si virgineum suffuderit ore ruborem,/ventus erit*.

V EXPLOITS (πράξεις). **428-618.** This section is used to recount the
deeds of the person being praised, arranged in such a way as to show the
qualities that underlie them. All rhetorical teaching on the subject agrees

that the cardinal virtues — bravery, justice, moderation, wisdom — should be indicated. Menander (*R.G.* 3.373) makes a distinction between exploits in war and exploits in peace, and Claudian conforms to this pattern. Honorius' youth (he is still only fourteen) and his general lack of distinction place Claudian under severe constraints. He extricates himself from the difficulty by devoting a large part of this section to the campaigns of Stilicho and by claiming some of the credit for Honorius by the suggestion that he was the driving force behind them:

> hunc tamen in primis populos lenire feroces
> et Rhenum pacare *iubes*   (439-440)

>   post otia Galli
> limitis *hortaris* Graias fulcire ruinas   (459-460)

In this way Honorius is allowed a share in his general's bravery. The justice of Honorius is dealt with in 488-512, while wisdom is the quality hinted at in 513-17. A panegyric must also include some praise of the subject's physical qualities, and this is found in 518-64, where beauty of form (518-28), strength (527-38) and speed and horsemanship (539-64) are described. The section ends with a picture of Honorius, magnificently attired, carried in state through crowds of his adoring subjects on the occasion of his arrival in Mediolanum during his second consulship in 394. Power and magnificence are the dominant notes.

428-429. aspice nunc, quacumque micas: Theodosius now dead has taken his place among the stars. His apotheosis is also described in *III Cons. Hon.* 162ff. Claudian invites him to look from heaven at the fulfilment of all his hopes for Honorius.

circulus Austri ... gelidi ... Triones: i.e. South and North. The *Triones* are the northern constellations of Ursa Maior and Ursa Minor. Cf. *lacteus ... circulus* of the Milky Way, at *VI Cons. Hon.* 174.

432. subnixus Stilichone tuo, quem fratribus ipse: this, like 315, 509, 635-36, is one of the verses restored by Bentinus in the edition of Isengrinius (Basel, 1534) and occurs in no ms. now extant. The introduction of Stilicho by the words *clipeum defensoremque* (433) and the absence of his name before 459 in a passage in which he is the central figure would be intolerably awkward.

Stilicho, a soldier of Vandal extraction, was the husband of Serena, niece and adopted daughter of the emperor Theodosius, who towards the end of his life appointed him *magister militum* in the West. The link with the Imperial house was later strengthened by the marriage of his daughter, Maria, to Honorius. His importance in the situation created by the death of Theodosius was quickly realised by Claudian, who devoted a large part of his literary output to championing the claims and promoting the designs of Stilicho. These poems were collected, most probably at Stilicho's command, and were transmitted separately from the rest of Claudian's work under the name of *Claudianus maior*.

Claudian repeatedly insists on Stilicho's claim (Zosimus 5.4: see note on 432-433 below) that to him belonged the tutelage both of Honorius in the West and of Arcadius in the East, and labours the point to such an extent as to make the claim seem dubious and tendentious. In support of Stilicho Claudian castigated Rufinus and Eutropius, the ministers of Arcadius. In 397 the tension was such that Stilicho was declared *hostis publicus* by Arcadius, though Claudian in this and his other poems contrives to give the impression that what bad blood there was subsisted at ministerial level only and did not affect the relationship between the imperial brothers. This was the state of affairs obtaining when Claudian composed this poem towards the end of 397. It will be noted that he does not here allude to the assassination of Rufinus in 395, for which Claudian gives Stilicho full credit (*In Ruf.* 2.402: for an assessment of Stilicho's motives and Claudian's attitude thereto, see Cameron, *Claudian*, pp.63ff. and 159ff.; also Döpp, *loc.cit.*, pp.61ff. and 88ff.). Equally there is no allusion here to the fact that the East had formally declared Stilicho a *hostis publicus*, nor to current Western misgivings about the attitude of Constantinople to Gildo and the possibility of their mounting armed intervention to support him against Rome. *Concordia fratrum* was therefore important to Rome at this juncture.

432-433. quem fratribus ipse/discedens clipeum defensorem dedisti: for this claim, see preceding note and cf. especially *III Cons. Hon.* 153-54:

> tu curis succede meis, tu pignora solus
> nostra fove: geminos dextra tu protege fratres.

But Claudian takes the precaution of making it clear that there were no witnesses to Theodosius' charge to Stilicho: *cunctos discedere tectis/dux iubet* (*III Cons. Hon.* 142f.). The exact interpretation of Theodosius' intentions and the construction to be placed on Claudian's references to Stilicho's role have been hotly disputed, notably by A. Cameron, *Claudian*, pp.37ff. and 'Theodosius and the regency of Stilico', *HSCPh.* 73 (1969) pp.247ff. He states (*Claudian* p.40) that "when Claudian arrived at Milan some time in the course of 395, Stilico was engaged in trying to convince the world at large that Theodosius really had declared him regent of both Honorius and Arcadius". A recent perceptive appraisal of the situation is that by Döpp, *loc.cit.* pp.61ff., who notes a difference between the way in which Claudian refers to Stilicho's role in *III Cons. Hon.* (composed towards the end of 395) and in the later poems which refer to it (*In Ruf.*, *Epith. Hon.*, *Stil.*). The language employed in *III Cons. Hon.* 152ff., taken in conjunction with Ambrose *De obitu Theodosii* 5 (*de filiis . . . nihil habebat quod conderet, quibus totum dederat, nisi ut eos* praesenti *commendaret* parenti), suggests to Döpp that Theodosius' "deathbed settlement" was limited to a commendation of both sons to the fatherly care of Stilicho, and did not extend to formal regency. A more extended brief is claimed for Stilicho from about 396 on: thus *Romana potentia, rerum . . . apex* (*In Ruf.* 2.4f.); *leges . . . et rerum . . . habenae* (*Epith. Hon.* 307f.); *commissis . . . terris* (*Stil.* 1.141). The fact that from this date onwards Stilicho permits himself to be referred to by Claudian as though he had actually been appointed regent by Theodosius denotes a reinterpretation of his role in the light of his *de facto* position and a reappraisal of Theodosius' original charge.

436-438. Libyae ... Syrtes: Claudian instances only Africa as a possible theatre of action for Stilicho, where he might, had he been praising Stilicho in general terms, have indulged in one of his favourite north/south, hot/ cold antitheses. The exclusively African reference here, like the suppression of the name of Africa at 391-93 above and 639-40 below, must carry a strong hint of action contemplated against Gildo at the time when Claudian was writing, if indeed the expedition to Africa was not actually under way. The expedition, when it happened, was led not by Stilicho, but by Gildo's brother Mascezel, though in a later account of the Gildonic war Claudian alleges that Stilicho was ready with a back-up force if needed: *si quid licuisset iniquis/casibus, instabant aliae post terga biremes;/venturus dux maior erat* (*Stil.* 1.366ff.). See further Cameron, *Claudian*, pp.114 and 119.

437-438. madidaque cadente/Pleiade: the Pleiads rise in May and set in September, and until their rising navigation was normally suspended (Hesiod, *O.D.* 618ff.).

(a) 439-487. War: Stilicho's expeditions to the Rhine and the Peloponnese.

439-459. The campaign of Stilicho along the Rhine frontier appears from Claudian's accounts (it is described again in *Stil.* 1.188ff.) to have been an entirely bloodless affair and the likeliest explanation is that it was a recruiting campaign: *quotiens sociare catervas/oravit iungique tuis Alamannia signis* (*Stil.* 1.232f.). Claudian is the sole authority for this mission and the present passage (*in primis . . . lenire . . . iubes*) has raised the presumption that it took place soon after Theodosius' death and in the same year, 395 (thus J. Koch, 'Claudian und die Ereignisse der Jahr 395 bis 398', *Rheinisches Museum*, 44, 1889, pp.575ff.). As it is not mentioned in either *III Cons. Hon.* or *In Ruf.*, it seems better to assume that it actually took place in 396. See Döpp *loc.cit.* p.103 and note 5.

440. iubes: see introduction to this section.

449. supplex Alamannia: cf. the passage from *Stil.* 1 quoted in note to 439-459 above.

450. Bastarnae: the name of the tribes (for which see OCD^2) are, of course, used more for effect than from considerations of historical relevance or geographical accuracy. Thus the Bastarnae would seem at this time to be settled in *Dacia Ripensis*: C.J. Simpson, 'Claudian and the federation of the Bastarnae', *Latomus*, 34 (1976) pp.221ff.

452. Albim liquere Cherusci: the Cherusci were more closely associated with the Weser than the Elbe: A. Loyen, 'L'*Albis* chez Claudien et Sidoine Apollinaire', *Revue des Etudes Latines*, 11 (1933) pp.203ff.

455. nobilitant veteres Germanica foedera Drusos: Nero Claudius Drusus, brother of the emperor Tiberius, who conducted important campaigns against the Germans (12-9 B.C.) and his son Germanicus Caesar, sent in A.D. 14 to quell the rising amongst the Gallic legions.

459-483. Stilicho's second expedition to Greece can be confidently dated to 397. It follows an earlier mission to Greece in 395, described in *In Ruf.* 2, when, evidently in compliance with an instruction from the Eastern court, he detached his own forces and retired before he had any chance to engage the Goths. But for this, Claudian maintains, Alaric would not have been left free to overrun the Peloponnese (*In Ruf.* 2.186ff.) as he did in 396-7. Zosimus (5.4-7) describes how Alaric and his forces poured through Thermopylae and would have stormed Athens had he not been deterred by a vision of Athena Promachos. Corinth was burned and Argos and Sparta presented no difficulty. In 397, Stilicho crossed by sea to the Isthmus of Corinth and pursued Alaric to Mt. Pholoe in Arcadia, on the frontiers of Elis, near the mouths of the Peneus. As in most of Stilicho's actions, victory eluded him when it seemed within his grasp, and Alaric escaped from the blockade. Zosimus attributes the failure to the indisciplined behaviour of Stilicho's troops, Claudian (as in 395) to the treachery of the Eastern Government (*Bell. Get.* 516f.). (It should be noted that Zosimus confuses the expeditions of 395 and 397.)

464-465. puer ... cum matre Palaemon: Palaemon (originally called Melicertes) and his mother Ino (Leucothea) were turned into sea-deities. The Isthmean games were instituted in his honour.

467-470. Lycaei ... Erymantheae ... Maenala: wooded uplands in Arcadia. The cutting down of forests is an epic commonplace: cf. Homer *Il.* 23.114ff.; Ennius, *A.* 187ff. Vahlen^2; Virg. *Aen.* 6,179, etc.

471. excutiat cineres Ephyre: Ephyre was an ancient name of Corinth, which was burnt during Alaric's passage: see note on 459-483 above and *In Ruf.* 2.190 and *Bell. Goth.* 612. Claudian is, of course, thinking of the phoenix, to which he devotes 110 verses in *c.m.* 27; cf. also *Stil.* 1.186f.: *resurgens/aegra caput mediis erexit Graecia flammis.*

479. uno colle: Pholoe (Zosimus 5.7).

485-487. Sarmata ... Gelonus ... Alani: the *Notitia Dignitatum* (pp. 218f.) shows the Sarmatae widely dispersed throughout Gaul and Italy. The Alani entered Europe in the wake of the Sarmatae, eventually settling in Spain where they were absorbed by the Visigoths. The Geloni are said to have assisted Theodosius against Eugenius (*Bell. Gild.* 245). All three tribes, however, now allegedly embracing Honorius' rule, are represented as having fought against Stilicho in the inconclusive battle at the Hebrus, 392 (*In Ruf.* 1.308ff.). So Claudian rounds off the warlike side of Honorius' reign.

(b) 488-517. Peace: Honorius' justice (488-512); his wisdom (513-517).

488. fortes ... animisque paratos: cf. Sallust *Cat.* 58.8, *moneo uti forti atque parato animo sitis*; Virg. *Aen.* 2.799, *animisque parati.*

489. sic iustos in pace legis: Claudian, constrained by Honorius' lack of achievement, is reduced virtually to adapting the words of the rhetorical instructions for this section: Menander (*R.G.* 3.375), ἐρεῖς ὅτι δικαίους ἄρχοντας ... ἐκπέμπει φύλακας τῶν νόμων καὶ τῆς τοῦ βασιλέως δικαιοσύνης ἀξίους, οὐ συλλογέας πλούτου ... ("you will say that he sends out just governors, guardians of the laws and fit agents of the royal justice, not collectors of wealth ...").

492-493. bellatore Quirino/ ... placido ... Numa: *ita duo deinceps reges ... ille bello, hic pace civitatem auxerunt* (Livy 1.21.6).

496. impia continui cessant augmenta tributi: here again Claudian is following closely the advice of Menander (*loc.cit.* at 489).

497. infelices tabulae: lists of proscribed persons and the properties confiscated.

497-498. non hasta refixas/vendit opes: avida sector non voce citatur: "No sales of forfeit goods beneath the spear: no buyer is summoned by the voice of greed." A spear planted in the ground was the sign that an auction was in progress from early Republican days (Livy 5.16.7). The right of the magistrate to sell goods seized in satisfaction of debts to the exchequer was called *ius hastae* (Tacitus *A.* 13.28.5). *refixas* is probably unique in the sense of 'forfeited'. *avida* is transferred from the motive for the sale to the voice of the auctioneer (*praeco*): cf. Cic. *Phil.* 2.64, *bona ... voci acerbissimae subiecta praeconis. sector: sectores vocantur qui publica bona mercantur* (Gaius, *Inst.* 4.146).

501-502. perdurat non empta fides nec pectora merces/adligat: cf. 120f. above: *hinc [sc. a Theodosio] amor, hinc validum devoto milite robur./ hinc natis mansura fides.* On this question of loyalty, see Cameron, *Claudian*, pp.171f.

503. te miles nutritor amat: cf. 150ff. above, *exercitus undique fulgens adstitit* etc.

504. quam fixa manet reverentia patrum: Claudian makes much of the fact that senatorial approval was sought for the war against Gildo: *neglectum Stilicho per tot iam saecula morem/rettulit ut ducibus mandarent proelia patres* (*Stil.* 1.329f.).

505-506. senium ... canitem: *senium* denotes the decrepitude of old age, *canities* its venerable qualities, hence "authority". Thus at *Manl. Theod.* 19, *canities animi* means "maturity of mind".

508. Pandioniae: "Athenian", from Pandion, an early king.

508-509. Lacedaemon ... Lycurgo: Lycurgus had forbidden Sparta to be defended with walls; cf. Livy 39.37.1-3. *Lacedaemon:* the quadrisyllabic ending is rare in Claudian.

516. linguae modus: it would have been difficult to ascribe eloquence to the youth, so his want of it is neatly turned into a compliment.

(c) **518-564.** Physical attributes: beauty (518-519); strength (520-538); speed (539-564).

518-519. torva voluptas ... augusti ... pudoris ... maiestas grata: the threefold oxymoron shows Claudian at his most precious and affected.

520. patrias imples galeas: so Proserpine, *nunc crinita iubis galeam, laudante Minerva,/implet, Rapt. Pros.* 3.219f. Cf. Stat. *Theb.* 8.292f.: *visusque ... nec adhuc inplere tiaram.*

520-521. cornus avita/temptatur: Stat. *Ach.* 1.41, *patria iam se metitur in hasta.*

522. Romanaque vota moratur: the promise of an *ingens dextra* held out by Honorius' early exercises raises impatient wishes for its fulfilment. Cf. Horace *Epist.* 1.1.23f., *ingrataque tempora, quae spem ... morantur* *agendi*; Claud. *Epith. Hon.* 20f., *quorum usque verendus/cunctatur mea vota socer?*

524. **casside maior**: made even taller by the helmet.

525-526. **Threicia ... in hasta ... Martem**: Thrace is the home of Mars, as Cyprus is of Venus; thus Ovid *A.A.* 2.587 (imitating Homer *Od.* 8.361), *Mars Thracem occupat, illa Paphum.*

527-528. **Gortynia ... spicula**: Gortyn, like Cydonia (530), a Cretan city. Cretan archery was famous: cf. Virg. *Aen.* 11.773, *spicula ... Gortynia.* Armenians and Parthians were equally celebrated.

530. **Cydon**: a native of Cydonia.

531. **refugo ... Partho**: so called from their trick of shooting back when in retreat: cf. *III Cons. Hon.* 201f., *Parthumque coactum/non ficta trepidare fuga.* See Nisbet-Hubbard on Hor. *Odes* 1.19.11.

532-536. **Amphioniae ... palaestrae ... Alcides ... Dircaeaque tela ... Gigantes ... Alcmenae**: Thebes, of which Amphion was king, was where Alcmena bore Hercules (Alcides) by Jupiter. The spring Dirce was in the neighbourhood. Hercules, using arrows, joined forces with Jupiter to defeat the Giants: see Pindar *Pyth.* 8.19, and Apollodorus 1.6.2.

537. **caeruleus tali prostratus Apolline Python**: snakes are commonly so described: cf. Virg. *Geo.* 4.482, *caeruleosque ... angues.* A similar comparison is found in *Ecl. Einsied.* 1.32: *talis Phoebus erat cum laetus caede draconis....* Arrows were once again the weapons used (Ovid *Met.* 1.441ff.).

539. **simulacraque Martia**: Lucr. 2.41, *belli simulacra.*

542. **Massagetae**: a Scythian tribe mentioned often for their custom of drinking horses' blood: so *In Ruf.* 1.310f.

543. **bimembres**: the Centaurs, as at Virg. *Aen.* 8,293.

544. **alae**: "squadrons" but with the idea of wings in mind.

545. **ferventesque tument post terga dracones**: these dragon standards that inflated in the wind are much liked by Claudian: cf. *III Cons. Hon.* 138f.; *In Ruf.* 2.176ff.; *VI Cons. Hon.* 565ff. Vegetius 2.13 says they were the standard of a cohort. For illustration, see Daremberg-Saglio art. *signa militaria* p.1321[1].

552-553. **solem/combibit**: Juvenal 11.203, *nostra bibat vernum contracta cuticula solem.*

554-564. **si dominus legeretur equis ...**: Claudian is reversing an idea of Statius *Silv.* 1.1.54f.: the great horse of Domitian will *not* change its rider.

555. **Nereidum stabulis nutritus Arion**: Arion was sired by Neptune and was the horse of Adrastus, one of the "Seven against Thebes".

556. **Castore**: Castor has the epithet ἱππόδαμος ("tamer of horses") in Homer.

557. **flavum Xanthus sprevisset Achillem**: Xanthus is the horse that warned Achilles of his death in *Il.* 19.404-424. ξάνθος = *flavus*: hence the juxtaposition.

560. **Bellerophonteas**: the adjective, filling two and a half feet, is borrowed from Propertius 3.3.2. Rutilius Namatianus used it to complete a

pentameter in two words: *Bellerophonteis sollicitudinibus* (1.450).

(d) 565-618. Honorius' entry into Mediolanum in 394.

The passage that follows is not a mere resumption of the description of the *processus consularis* of 398, with which Claudian opened the poem, though this is the interpretation sometimes placed on it (e.g. Averil Cameron, *loc.cit.* at 5-17 above, p.202: "*IV Cos. Hon.* 1f., 565f. describes the procession of Honorius in Milan in 397 [*sic*]"). In 394 after his victory over Eugenius, Theodosius summoned Honorius from Constantinople to Mediolanum: see 391-392 and note. The journey, which Honorius made in the company of Serena (*VI Cons. Hon.* 88-100), his sister by adoption, wife of Stilicho, and later his mother-in-law, is described in *III Cons. Hon.* 111-125 and is followed by an account of the entry into Mediolanum, 126-141. It provided invaluable material for the πράξεις section of that poem. The point of the present passage is correctly taken by Döpp, *loc.cit.* pp.117f. What Claudian is now describing is an *adventus*, the arrival of a ruler or other person of great importance: see Sabine MacCormack, 'Change and continuity in Late Antiquity: The Ceremony of *Adventus*', *Historia*, 21 (1972) pp.721ff., who, however, refers the passage to the *processus consularis* of 398. Since Honorius was, in fact, consul for the year of his *adventus* in Mediolanum in 394, his regalia and attendance were doubtlessly identical with those of the *processus consularis*.

566. Ausonio ... amictu: the *trabea*, also called *Quirinali ... amictu* (157) and *Romuleo ... amictu* (*In Eutr.* 2.62).

567. per Ligurum populos: Mediolanum, at this time the capital of the Western empire, had been the seat of the governor of Liguria since 300. For Claudian's avoidance of the name, see note on 17 above.

568. inter niveas ... cohortes: cf. 7, *discolor ... legio* and 9-10, *togatus/miles*.

569. pubes electa: cf. Corippus *Laus Iustini* 4.228ff.: *gratoque labori/submittunt umeros et loris fortibus aptant/electi iuvenes.*

570-571. sic numina Memphis/in vulgum proferre solet: Claudian, as a native of Alexandria, may well have witnessed the ceremonies he now describes: for similar Egyptian allusions and reminiscences, see Birt, *introd.* pp.iff. especially p.v. "The allusion is to an Egyptian festival celebrated at the winter solstice, when the statue of a small boy representing the Sun at its lowest point, when the days are beginning to get longer, was carried from a shrine" (MacCormack, *loc.cit.* p.737). The sun-symbolism (see note on 121 above) implied in the allusion is noteworthy. The significance of this passage was first explained by E. Norden, *Die Geburt des Kindes*, (Leipzig, 1924) p.25 n.3.

572. brevis illa quidem: as indeed the ten-year-old consul must have been.

573. liniger ... sacerdos: similarly Ovid *Met.* 1.747, *nunc dea linigera colitur celeberrima turba*, and Juvenal 6.532, *grege linigero circumdatus.*

574. testatus sudore deum: weight was one of the signs of divinity and the idea became a commonplace, especially in regard to the apotheosis of a

dead emperor: cf. Lucan 1.53ff., and *III Cons. Hon.* 108 (of Theodosius), *nutaretque oneris venturi conscius Atlas.* Juvenal 13.47ff. speaks of an age when: contentaque sidera paucis
            numinibus miserum urguebant Atlanta minori
            pondere.

574-576. sistris . . . tibia: the rattle and the tibia were much used in the cult of Isis: cf. Tibullus 1.3.23f. and Apuleius *Met.* 11.9.

576. Apis: the sacred bull of Memphis, "the image of the soul of Osiris", Plutarch, *De Iside et Osiride* 20, 29 and 43.

577. tua sacra: as though Honorius were actually a god like Isis.

580. numeroso consule: = *numerosis consularibus.*

582. Tagus: the inhabitants of Spain are mentioned first as a compliment to Honorius' Spanish origins, while Africa is not mentioned at all: see note on 391-392 above.

583-584. Gallia/doctis civibus: the schools of Gaul were famous at this time: Ausonius, *Professores Burdigalenses,* provides contemporary evidence of their excellence.

584-585. portatur iuvenum cervicibus aurea sedes: virtually repeating 569-570.

588. fulgor Hiberus: Spanish gold was famous in antiquity.

590. picturatumque metallis: i.e. covered with embroidered pictures in gold and silver thread, which Claudian delights in describing, like the work of Proserpine at *Rapt. Pros.* 1.246ff. and the *trabea* of Stilicho, *Stil.* 2.339ff.

591. multa glomerantur iaspide vultus: i.e. portraits worked in jasper and closely packed together: for this practice see *Stil.* 2.339ff.

592. Nereia baca: the pearl, for which the Red Sea was famous (*Rubri maris,* 600).

597-598. divitis algae/germina: Ausonius *Mosella* 69ff.: *cum virides algas, et rubra corallia nudat/aestus, et albentes concharum germina bacus.*

599-601. quis iunxit lapides ostro?: Claudian plays with the effect of pearls and precious stones on Tyrian purple (an idea much liked by Tibullus, e.g. 3.3.17f., *quidve in Erythraeo legitur quae litore concha/ tinctaque Sidonio murice lana iuvat?*; cf. also *id.* 2.4.27f.) and the description ends with a resounding tricolon: *tribuere colorem/Phoenices, Seres subtegmina, pondus Hydaspes.* For Chinese silks, cf. *III Cons. Hon.* 211, *dabant . . . vellera Seres,* and for India (represented by the Hydaspes) as a source of precious stones, *ibid.* 4, *dives Hydaspeis augescat purpura gemmis.*

602-610. The section on πράξεις ends with a comparison of Honorius with Bacchus. Rhetorical teaching (e.g. Menander *R.G.* 3.376) recommends that the πράξεις should be followed by a separate section devoted to a general comparison of the whole reign of the subject with previous reigns (σύγκρισις τελειοτάτη). Claudian does not, however, either here or in his other encomia, follow this rule, preferring the "partial" comparison (σύγκρισις μερική), interspersed throughout the poem at appropriate places. For the other συγκρίσεις employed in this poem, see 132ff., 192ff., 197ff., 206ff., 374ff., 491ff., 507ff.

602. Maeonias ... per urbes: i.e. of Lydia — *Maeonia ante appellata* (Pliny *H.N.* 5.30.1).

603. pampineos ... thyrsos: the ivy-clad staff or spear carried by Bacchus and his devotees; Euripides *Bacchae* 25, κίσσινον βέλος; Virg. *Aen.* 7.396, *pampineas ... hastas.*

604-605. Nysa ... tigres: Nysa, of uncertain location, was a mountain-haunt of Bacchus; Virg. *Aen.* 6.805, *Liber agens celso Nysae de vertice tigres.*

606. talis Erythraeis intextus nebrida gemmis: Red Sea pearls again. *intextus nebrida* is middle with direct object as in 608 below, *crinemque solutae.* The fawnskin was as closely associated with Bacchus and his followers as the thyrsus: Euripides *Bacchae* 24, νεβρίδ᾽ ἐξάψας χροός.

607. Liber: an old Italian deity of planting and fructification later identified with Bacchus.

Caspia/colla: "the necks of Caspian tigers". Hyrcania on the Caspian Sea was noted for its tigers.

608-610. Satyri ... Maenades ... Indos ... Ganges: Claudian has in mind Bacchus' progress through the East, for which see Euripides *Bacchae, init. Maenadës*: the female devotees of Bacchus.

611. quater: = *quartum.* Honorius' previous consulships were in 386, 394 and 396.

612-613. sollemnia ludit/omina libertas: the custom of manumitting slaves on the consul's taking up office is referred to again by Claudian at *In Eutr.* 1.309f., *praebet miracula lictor/consule nobilior libertatemque daturus,/quam necdum meruit*; also Sidon. Apoll. *Pan. Anthem. dict.* 544ff. It is not clear when the custom began, but its inclusion in the inauguration ceremonies is easy to understand: the manumission of the slave Vindicius (see on 613) was one of the earliest events to take place after the office of consul was instituted in 509 B.C., and, as an act of bounty, it made a good omen.

613. Vindice: his name according to Livy was actually Vindicius. He disclosed the plot to restore the Tarquins and was given his freedom in reward (Livy 2.5). The rod used to administer the token blow (*ictu*, 615) of manumission was called *vindicta* or *festuca.* The slave was also given a slap (*alapa*) as described in 616-17, and finally turned around by his late owner: Persius 5.78, *verterit hunc dominus, momento turbinis exit/ Marcus Dama.* See R.G. Nisbet, 'Festuca and Alapa of Manumission', *JRS* 8 (1918) 1ff.

VI EPILOGUE (ἐπίλογος). **619-656.** The victories won in Honorius' previous consulships augur well for the fourth. The poet prays that he may be consul for ever and looks forward to Honorius' marriage, and to the subjugation of all lands and peoples from North to East under the joint fasces of Honorius and Arcadius.

In attributing Theodosius' victories to Honorius' consular auspices,

Claudian employs again the device he used in the πράξεις section (see introd. to § V). The use of the prayer is recommended by Aphthonius (*R.G.* 2.36) and Menander (*R.G.* 3.377).

620. in nomen ventura tuum: i.e. *in annum qui tuo nomine in fastis signabitur.*

622. totiens accessit laurea patri: Claudian's examples are the defeat of the Gruthungi in 386 (623-633) and the overthrow of Eugenius in 394. He is unable to point to anything of significance in the third consulship in 396, a year that saw the unchecked progress of Alaric downwards into Greece.

623-633. The attempt of the Gruthungi, an Ostrogothic tribe led by Odothaeus, to cross the Danube is described by Zosimus (4.38f.). The chronicles of Idatius and Marcellinus place it in 386. They add that Theodosius and Arcadius celebrated a triumph for it in Constantinople. Zosimus (4.39.4) alleges that Theodosius appeared on the scene only after his lieutenant Promotus had secured the victory. See further F. Paschoud, *Zosime*, vol. 4^2, Paris (1979) p.410 note 169.

624. in lintres fregere nemus: Zosimus 4.38.5, πλήθει μονοξύλων ἐμβιβάσαντες; but he does not mention the number 3,000. They were evidently some kind of canoe or one-man raft.

629. Arctoos pavere cadavera pisces: Plautus *Rudens* 513, *piscibus in alto . . . praebent pabula*, and often in Latin poetry.

630. Peuce: an island near the mouths of the Danube. It was the birthplace of Alaric: *VI Cons. Hon.* 105f., *Alaricum barbara Peuce/nutrierat.*

631. barbaricos vix egerat unda cruores: the panegyrist is encouraged to tell of rivers choked with corpses and running red: Menander *R.G.* 3.374, ἐρεῖς καὶ ὅτι ἐστενοχωρεῖτο τοῖς τῶν πεσόντων σώμασιν.... Zosimus (4.39.3) gives a similar description of the scene following the battle.

633-634. civile . . . bellum: the revolt of Eugenius; a very brief reference as the subject is almost played out by now.

639-640. semper venere triumphi/cum trabeis: with the tacit implication that the year will see a successful conclusion to the campaign against Gildo; see on 436-438 above. This time, however, Honorius will be the sole *auctor* (638) of the success.

641-642. Mariique relinquas/et senis Augusti numerum: Marius held the office seven times, Augustus thirteen. So Ausonius, *Grat. Act.* 6: *te videre saepius in hoc magistratu, Gratiane, desidero, ut et sex Valerii Corvini et septem C. Marii et cognominis tui Augusti tredecim consulatus aequipares.*

644-646. cum tibi protulerit festas nox pronuba taedas . . .: the marriage of Honorius to Maria, the daughter of Stilicho and Serena, took place in the early part of 398, not many weeks after the inauguration. Claudian contrives here to give the impression that a match for the emperor is still only a pious hope. This may be a discreet reticence on Claudian's part about a previously laid plan of Stilicho to strengthen his connection with the royal house by marrying the emperor to his daughter. The importance of such a union and the need to expedite it become clearer in the light of the events of late 397/early 398. In *Bell. Gild.* 286-88, Theodosius begs Arcadius not to be drawn into Civil War because of Gildo's defection from the West: *ne consanguineis certetur comminus armis,/ne, precor*. . . . The threat of Eastern armed intervention on behalf of Gildo was evidently a real one, and this is the purport of Theodosius' final plea to Arcadius (*Bell. Gild.* 314): *sed tantum permitte, cadat. nil poscimus ultra.* (See further Döpp *loc.cit.* 145f. and 148.) In the event of a defeat, Stilicho's position would have been very serious indeed. He, therefore, brought the marriage about at this time as a matter of urgency. Claudian's picture in *Epith. Hon.* of Honorius the ardent suitor being frustrated by Stilicho's objections to the match (20ff.) may be taken for what it is worth. Birt saw a veiled hint at the identity of the bride-to-be in the repetition of the syllable *MARI* in 641, 646 and 648 (p.xxxii note 4).

650-651. o mihi si liceat thalamis intendere carmen/conubiale tuis, si te iam dicere patrem: Claudian's first wish was granted and his next compositions were to include the *Fescennina de Nuptiis Honorii Augusti* and the *Epithalamium.* He was not so fortunate with his second wish. There was no issue from the match. According to Zosimus (5.28) Serena, out of regard for Maria's tender age, procured the services of a wise woman who contrived that, while Honorius shared her bed, he was both unable and unwilling to discharge the duties of a husband. In 407 Honorius married Thermantia, another daughter of Serena, Maria having died not long before: this marriage was shortlived and childless.

652. trans Rheni cornua: the word *cornu* is used of rivers that enter the sea by many mouths, like the Nile (Ovid, *Met.* 9.774) and river gods are regularly represented as having bulls' horns (Virg. *Geo.* 4.371; Claud. *P.O.* 221; *In Eutr.* 2.164).

653. spoliis Babylonis onustus: cf. Virg. *Aen.* 1.289, *spoliis Orientis onustum*, and see note on 655-656.

654. communem maiore toga signabitis annum: Arcadius and Honorius had been colleagues in the consulship in 394 and 396.

655. crinitusque tuo sudabit fasce Suevus: Tacitus (*Germ.* 38) notes the custom of this race to wear their hair in a style that distinguished them from other Germans. *fasce* may mean the soldier's pack or the consular insignia, though the singular noun is not very common in the latter sense (see *Thes. Ling. Lat. s.v. fascis*). Virgil (*Geo.* 3.347) and Pacatus (33.4) show the former meaning. On balance, in view of *maiore toga* (654) and *fraternas secures* (656), we should probably here understand *fasces*, with *Thes. Ling. Lat. In Eutr.* 1.380, 394, shows Honorius later in 398 entertaining a legation of the Suevi at Mediolanum and receiving their submission.

655-656. ultima . . . Bactra: the poem ends with another Virgilian echo (*Aen.* 8.687f., *ultima . . . Bactra*). Bactra (n.pl.) is the capital of Bactria. The epilogue to *III Cons. Hon.* (189-211) is constructed on lines very similar to this one, the names in the final prophecy being chosen to cover widely separated points of the brothers' dominion. The coupling of Bactra and Babylon in this context recalls the final lines of Janus' speech in Statius' poem on Domitian's seventeenth consulship: *restat Bactra novis, restat Babylona tributis/frenari* (*Silv.* 4.1.40f.).

SELECT BIBLIOGRAPHY

CLAUDIAN: complete works

Claudianus, *Carmina*, ed. T. Birt, Monumenta Germaniae Historica, auct. ant. vol. x, Berlin 1892.

Claudianus, *Carmina*, ed. J. Koch, Leipsig 1893.

Claudian, with an English translation, M. Platnauer, Loeb Classical Library, London and New York 1922.

CLAUDIAN: single works.

The In Eutropium of Claudius Claudianus, A.C. Andrews, Philadelphia, 1931.

Claudien, *Invectives contre Eutrope*, P. Fargues, Paris 1933.

Claudien, *Panegyricus de quarto consulatu Honorii Augusti*, P. Fargues, Aix-en-Province 1936.

Claudian, *De raptu Proserpinae*, J.B. Hall, Cambridge 1969.

Claudian's In Rufinum: an exegetical commentary, H.L. Levy, Cleveland 1971.

Claudians Festgedicht auf das sechste Konsulat des Kaisers Honorius, K.A. Müller, Berlin 1938.

Claudii Claudiani De bello Gildonico, E.M. Olechowska, Leiden 1978.

Claudians Gedicht vom Gotenkrieg, H. Schroff, Berlin 1927.

Claudiani panegyricus de consulatu Manlii Theodori, W. Simon, Berlin 1975.

OTHER AUTHORS

Chroniclers (Idatius, Marcellinus, Ravenna Chronicle): *Chronica Minora*, ed. T. Mommsen, M.G.H., auct. ant., vols. ix and xi, Berlin 1892, 1894.

Codex Theodosianus: *Theodosiani libri xvi*, ed. T. Mommsen and P.M. Meyer, Berlin 1905.

Ecclesiastical historians (Philostorgius, Socrates, Sozomen): Patrologia Graeca, ed. J.-P. Migne, Paris 1864: Philostorgius, vol. lxv; Socrates, Sozomen, vol. lxvii.

Notitia dignitatum utriusque imperii, ed. O. Seeck, Berlin 1876.

Pacatus: *XII Panegyrici Latini*, ed. R.A.B. Mynors, Oxford 1964.

Rhetoricians (Aphthonius, Menander): *Rhetores Graeci*, rec. L. Spengel: Aphthonius, vol. ii, Leipsig 1854; Menander, vol. iii, Leipsig 1856.

Zosimus, ed. L. Mendelssohn, Leipsig 1887.
    ed. and tr. F Paschoud, Paris 1971-1979.

OTHER WORKS

G. Boissier, *La fin du paganisme*, vol. ii, Paris 1891.

P. Brown, *The world of late antiquity*, London 1971.

J.B. Bury, *History of the later Roman empire from the death of Theodosius I to the death of Justinian*[2], vol. i, London 1923.

A. Cameron, *Claudian: poetry and propaganda at the court of Honorius*, Oxford 1970.

J.H.E. Crees, *Claudian as an historical authority*, Cambridge 1908.

E. Demougeot, *De l'unité à la division de l'empire romain 395-410*, Paris 1951.

S. Dill, *Roman Society in the last century of the western empire*[2], London 1899.

S. Döpp, *Zeitgeschichte in Dichtungen Claudians*, Wiesbaden 1980.[1]

P. Fargues, *Claudien: études sur sa poésie et son temps*, Paris 1933.

A.H.M. Jones, *The later Roman empire 284-602*, Oxford 1964.

O. Kehding, *De panegyricis latinis capita quattuor*, Marburg 1899.

H.L. Levy, 'Themes of encomium and invective in Claudian', *Transactions and Proceedings of the American Philological Association* 89 (1958) 336ff.

A. Lippold, *Theodosius der Grosse und seine Zeit*, Stuttgart 1968.

S. MacCormack, 'Change and continuity in late antiquity: the ceremony of *adventus*', *Historia* 21 (1972) 721ff.

S. Mazzarino, *Stilicone: la crisi imperiale dopo Teodosio*, Rome 1942.

F. Paschoud, *Roma Aeterna*, Institut Suisse de Rome 1967.

S. Perowne, *The end of the Roman world*, London 1966.

F.J.E. Raby, *Secular Latin poetry*[2], vol. i, Oxford 1957.

E. Stein, *Histoire du bas-empire*, vol. i, Bruges 1959.

L.B. Struthers, 'The rhetorical structure of the encomia of Claudius Claudian', *Harvard Studies in Classical Philology* 30 (1919) 49ff.

1. Contains an exhaustive and up-to-date bibliography.